CLIMBING THE SACRED MOUNTAIN

CLIMBING THE SACRED MOUNTAIN:
POEMS AND PRAYERS
OF A WESTERN YOGI

By Yogacharya David R. Hickenbottom

Edited by Ruth M. Lamb, Ph.D

The Cross and The Lotus Publishing
Camano Island, Washington, USA

Climbing the Sacred Mountain—Poems and Prayers of a Western Yogi
©2021, The Cross and the Lotus Publishing

All rights reserved. No part of this publication may, for commercial benefit, be reproduced, distributed, or transmitted in any form or by any means, including photocopying, recording, or other electronic or mechanical methods without the prior written permission of the publisher, except in the case of brief quotations embodied in critical reviews and certain other non-commercial uses permitted by copyright law.

For permission requests, contact the publisher at:
http://www.crossandlotus.com/contact.html

ISBN 978-1-7355535-3-5 (softcover)
ISBN 978-1-957811-15-4 (eBook)

First reprint, 2024

All photos courtesy David Hickenbottom Portfolio, with the exception of Arunachala Mountain, photo, Ruth Lamb.

The Expanding Path, photo, Michael Victory.

Mount Temple, painting, Dennis Brown.

Published by
The Cross and the Lotus Publishing
Camano Island, Washington, usa
Website: www.crossandlotus.com

Reverend David, On Mountain Path. 1989.

Contents

Preface	1
Introduction	5
Chapter One: The Call and The Response	21
Chapter Two: The Path of Purification	65
Chapter Three: The Path of Conscious Witnessing	115
Chapter Four: Homecoming	161
Chapter Five: Prayers	199
Chapter Six: Guru Tribute	215
Chapter Seven: India's Gifts	255
Chapter Eight: Mahasamadhi	277
Chapter Nine: Aphorisms and Principles	303
Chapter Ten: Closure	317
Acknowledgments	327
Index of Poems	329
Bibliography	335

Yogacharaya David at Sri Yukteswariji's Altar. India. 1998.

Preface

Reverend Yogacharya David Hickenbottom (1954–2019) was a disciple of Yogacharya Mother Hamilton (1904–1991). As a young man, David met Yogacharya Mother Hamilton and he realized at once that he had found his Guru Teacher. The seeker of many years, through a set of chance circumstances, found his teacher—and the Dharma search for God-realization had truly begun. David became a Reverend in 1984, and when Mother Hamilton left her body, she gave the title Yogacharya and her spiritual mantle to David. A new Dharma, a new mountain, and David said, "Yes."

David gave many talks—well over a thousand—until he left his body in 2019. He gave workshops, wrote blog posts, provided innumerable one-to-one meetings, and led multi-day workshops and retreats both in the US and Canada. He also recounted experiences in a series of private journals where most of these poems were discovered. David, to our great regret, was called to God much sooner than any of us would wish.

When David's wife, Carla, asked to meet with me the morning after David's Memorial, she requested that I organize David's work and teachings for publication. Without a breath, I said "Yes." Carla and I then met with Reverend Larry Koler and his wife Cate to briefly discuss this devotional project. David had spoken to me much earlier on several occasions about my working with him to publish his teachings. He specifically wanted me to reference some of his experiences by linking them to historical, scientific, and evolutionary processes that support the living dynamic sacred nature of our human condition in this amazing universe. May his presence ever guide this devotional work.

As I began to catalogue the materials Carla gave me, to my surprise and the surprise of many, we found that David wrote poetry. At times he was very prolific, and at other times he journaled more prose than poetry. David wrote regularly in his journals, in these documents he shares his journey up the steep, sometimes perilous and at other times glorious Mountain. Most of these poems were written in various different journals starting from 1978 to 2019.

I have placed the poems in themes and added dates when possible to show the dynamic cyclical process of his inner and outer spiritual journey. Very few words have been changed, punctuation has been added in places, and titles provided as required. A list of poems and dates is provided in the reference section.

The themes for this collection seemed to arise spontaneously. They are, *The Call and the Response*; *The Path to Purification*; *The Path to Witness Consciousness*; *Homecoming*; *Prayers*; *Guru Tribute*; *India's Gifts*; *Mahasamadhi*; *Aphorisms and Principles*, and *Closure*. Admittedly, as you will see, many poems could fit under various themes. In fact, I am certain that no two people would place them in exactly this order. I humbly submit this compilation with a prayer that David whispered guidance along the way.

David made many pilgrimages to India. He shared his 1998 pilgrimage to India in *My Spiritual India*, a book he completed just prior to leaving his body. Here in this book, poems from that pilgrimage and other India pilgrimages are included, and of course, poems from 1978 onward.

David wrote more poems in his early journals. In the later journals he shared his mountain climb more via narratives of his experiences. Future publications will feature these narratives, along with talks and other writings.

A Personal Note

Soon after David started teaching as a Yogacharya, he visited Vancouver, B.C. Canada to give a talk. My friend invited me to the talk. I also had been seeking a spiritual path that connected deeply to some sacred longing in my heart. A path that honored freedom and deep personal commitment. Books from the East had been my guide.

When I arrived, my friend introduced me to David. I then sat down on a couch with a few others and went into silence until the talk started. Soon David began an hour talk. He spoke of Mother Hamilton and Yogananda and the path of Kriya Yoga. As I listened, I felt a magnificent golden sphere form around me. Pure and brilliant gold. An experience never to happen before or after. The gold was fully around me and 'felt' about four feet away. I was 'held' in this sphere of light until the talk ended. We all said farewell, and home we went. I was silent. Silent. Somehow no words could speak this experience—until now. My mountain had arrived. I had a teacher, though with my skepticism very awake and aware, it took me four years to formally ask David if he would be my teacher. David said "Yes!" Human and Divine: the divine knew right away, the human took four years!

David's poems share his climb up the sacred mountain.

May his experiences awaken the great inner fire in your heart,
May your materialistic, mechanistic, habit-based, programmed, perceptually imprisoned creative truth break free,
May the truly human and divinely human sacred activate;
May your unique Mountain climb bring the highest and best forth to this beautiful planet.

Ruth Lamb, February 3, 2021
Vancouver, BC, Canada

OM TAT SAT

Himalayas, N. India. 2005.

Introduction

Throughout the ages, great Masters have spoken of the sacred climb to access Divine-realization, to bring humanity in touch with the highest truth of existence. Yogacharya David Hickenbottom, even as a child, knew there was more than surface life. He sought via the church and through science and philosophy for answers. Then he found a teacher who spoke a new language, one of such deep inner awareness that a whole new world of freedom began unfolding. With his guide, David now starts his sacred climb in earnest. Here he shares his climb and the life experiences he undergoes through poems.

To place his explorations as he climbs in context, we begin with a quote from David's *Cloud Mountain Journal* as he reaches a plateau and follow with a brief outline of his life as he writes it up until 2007.

David reflects:

> My life is a dedication to God. In fumbling steps and in precision of movement I steer my life toward that precious Goal. My Great Guru set the course, direction and Goal. She beckons me still from her deeper life. God awakened me to that purpose when my own will would have taken me down to self-destruction, or, at best, to a mundane, senseless life. I pretend no greatness nor even goodness, for there is none other good than my Heavenly Father. Truly I can say wholeheartedly that it is by God and Guru's Grace that I have found my Self.
>
> I suppose it is natural to want all the world to share the sacred mystery that I feel, and it would be sheer arrogance to assume that no others do. But there is the song-bird within that bursts into Divine verse that aches to share that deepest Intimacy, yet finds that longing all the more painful as its song disappears into the void. The pain is nothing but God's

constant yearning for His children to forsake their gloom-drenched dream of creation long enough to join once again in Divine Union. Songs of Angels are not just beautiful voices, but the thrill of vibration that resounds throughout all space and is caught and finds resonance in the receptive soul.

David's poem, *I AM,* gives us an entry into the complexities, challenges and beauty of his climb to the heights over approximately forty-five years of the internal spiritual work that is sadhana.

I AM

In the beginning: I AM.
I was in the stars—the black sky—vast space—so free.
Then I thought, What would it be like to be part of the earth?
Five outer shells surrounded me, and I became earth!
I was red-hot lava: moving, flowing out of the earth—liquid rock.
I cooled—I became solid, hard rock! I was content to be rock and mountain for a very, very long time.
I was aware of growing things on the surface, roots reached down into my earth.
I thought, What is it like to be plant?
The outer shell of mineral dropped away—I became plant!
I was seed—seed stretched out into root—root yearned for light and became branch—branch broadened into leaf!
Life became more active—shorter—juicy and vibrant.
I lived as so many plants—green vines and ferns—I became bright flowers and rose into monarchs of the forest: giant trees.
So many varieties—always reaching for light.
Then I was aware of moving things: insects, worms, deer and bear.
The outer coating of vegetation dropped off and I became animal.
I swam in the sea—I burrowed in the ground—I flew in the sky.
I ran over hills—I drank cool water and ate berries with delight.
I discovered movement, experienced sight and sound through the senses.
I was sometimes frightened and ran! I was sometimes courageous and fought!

Change happened more quickly now—I learned to adapt.
So many experiences—so many changes—the good times and bad were higher and lower now.
Oh—so many forms of animals I tried on—so many lives I lived!
Then I became aware of human—I somehow knew this was the next step.
After my last life as animal, animal dropped off—I discovered higher centers of thought and awareness—even more possibilities.
I became—human!
Now I walked on two legs—my spine went up and down—not sideways like my animal body.
Language was more complicated—and ideas—more ideas—interesting ideas—also more confusing ideas that fought with each other.
And choices—more choices—I entered this human body with a greater desire to learn—learn about the power to choose—choose what I ate—who my friends were—creating good habits—and bad!
Life became more complex—more interesting.
And through my choices—my free will—I sometimes had pleasure—and sometimes pain—what I did, choices I made—brought pleasure or pain.
And oh what a maze—good and bad—high and low—I had the delight of figuring something out! Sometimes I had painful confusion.
As time went on I made better choices—I realized that how I treated myself—how I treated others—made a difference in whether I felt happy or sad.
After a very long time I became aware that I could become more—more than human.
I struggled to learn—to go to the next stage of evolution—but this time instead of a change of body—this required a change of mind, involution.
I was taught to quiet the mind.
When I learned to quiet the mind, the human covering fell away and those higher centers lit up—like a Christmas tree!
Now I re-membered who I was before the lava flow—the plant—

the animal—or even before I was human.
I remembered who and what I had always been—before all this activity—all of these bodies—all of this confusion!
The I, who had always been the same inside all those bodies—the I that was in the stars—the black sky—vast space—and so free!
The I AM that existed before even the stars—the I AM that is pure joy, love and Light!
The I AM that touches and is a part of everything that is!
The same I AM that is inside of you!
Finally, that last covering dropped off and I knew, I knew the forever
I AM
I knew God

David poetically shares that he 'knew' that he could become more than human, that he could take the human condition to the next stage of its evolution as has been taught by great Masters throughout the ages.

In 2007, David wrote a biographical sketch. He told the story of a young man in search of something of vaster more meaning than he had so far discovered. Excerpts from this sketch place his poems in context as he takes us with him on his magnificent challenging journey up the sacred mountain. The full biography can be found on The Cross and The Lotus web site at www.crossandlotus.com.

David speaks of coming into this world:

> It is not unusual for a yogi to have early memories or have them come spontaneously when in deepened meditation. My earliest memories come from being in the womb of my mother. One day as I was thinking about God, I felt a powerful force come over me and I spontaneously curled up in a fetal position. As I lay in a tight ball I had the experience of being in my mother's dark womb; I could hear her heart beating loudly. I was warm, comfortable, and it was soothing to be there. I enjoyed the experience and was content to be where I was. On the frontiers of my consciousness I was aware that I would eventually be born into the world. I was not looking forward to this and preferred to stay

> where I was. I knew my coming life would have great challenges, and my mother's womb was a comfort.
>
> At another time I had a spontaneous memory of my pre-birth life. I was with my astral family on an exceptionally beautiful astral planet. My parents were wonderfully wise, loving, joyful and light-filled beings and I loved them with all my heart. I knew I was coming to the earth for an incarnation and I knew it would be difficult. These wise beings assured me that I would be helped by someone who was tremendous during this life. While having this vision I knew they were speaking of my guru, Mother Hamilton.

David goes on to relate how he, as a child and young man, sought for more meaning in life both in church and through studying science. When they came up short he was then directed to study philosophy. Still his questions were not answered.

Then came an opening to the greater mystery:

> Finally it came to a head when I was nineteen years old. I remember sitting under the stars on a warm summer's night; it was around midnight. The stars were spread like a carpet of tiny lights above; my heart felt like it was physically breaking right down the middle. I felt a crushing weight pressing down on me and I was breaking under the strain. It was all too much for me and I made a spontaneous prayer in my agony, Oh God, I don't know if you exist, but if you do, if I have never needed you before, I need you now. Help me! Amazingly, with that prayer came an instant relief. I felt that a thousand pounds of weight came off of me in that moment. The tremendous pain in my heart was soothed. I was aware that in a split second, the agony I had been feeling was gone.
>
> Immediately after this unseen help came to my aid, my mind began to reason, Well, since I prayed to God, my mind imagined getting some help and I felt relief as a result, it was my mind, not anything else that helped me. Coming on the heels of this thought some gnosis,

a knowing, came to me and said, No, it was more than the mind. I connected with something wonderful and powerful and definitely beyond me. This was the beginning of my long road back.

David had other search experiences but here we focus on his being invited to a talk by a wise 'grandmother.' David says, "well, this grandmother description did not appeal to me. But . . . eventually I said yes."

On a Wednesday evening in the month of March, 1974, we all piled into a car and drove to a nice home in North Seattle . . . Mother began to speak with such spiritual power that I felt as if my long hair was being blown straight back. She spoke of God, of Self-realization, Christ-consciousness and renunciation. Many of the concepts were foreign to me, but I recognized that this was someone who spoke with authority and wisdom. After the talk, Mother gave each one of us a hug. As I stood in line waiting, getting one person closer to Mother, my heart was beating so hard I could feel it loudly thumping in my chest. After I hugged Mother I remember little until I found myself sitting in the back seat of the car I had come in . . . Each time I would come to hear Mother speak I would wonder if I would feel the same power of God, and each time it proved itself true . . . Before meeting Mother I would be looking for the nearest exit if someone started speaking about God, but when Mother used the word I knew there was a new and enlarged meaning.

David speaks of his initiation into Kriya Yoga that spring. He says, "I felt I had the means for making spiritual progress, something I could take with me everywhere." He had fully committed to sadhana, a Sanskrit name for spiritual practice. He goes on to say, "How I made contact with one of the greatest Masters this world has ever seen is a great mystery to me. Every day I thank the heavens for this greatest of gifts, a sense of gratitude that does not diminish with time, but only grows sweeter."

The Reverend Mother Yogacharya Mildred Hamilton (1904–1991) met Paramhansa Yogananda (1893–1952) whom she called 'Master,' in 1925. At that time she had been seeking deeper meaning in her life and spiritual guidance towards a truth she intuited was available but hidden from our daily view. Her first meeting with Master was in Seattle, Washington, USA. David said: "At that meeting, when Master looked at Mother she experienced a shock that went through her entire being."

Over time, Mother Hamilton became a Center Leader, then a Reverend, and finally in front of thousands, Mother Hamilton received the title Yogacharya from Yogananda. She was the only woman to receive this honor, and one of seven in total in his world-wide organization.

Yogananda followed the great Kriya lineage from India that came through Jesus, Babaji, Lahiri Mahasaya, and then Sri Yukteswar who was Yogananda's teacher. Yogananda created a large organization in America. His aim was to "bring all into the spiritual heights he enjoyed in God." And as David says: "This is the work of a spiritual master. A true master makes you feel as if God is very close, very intimate, and very knowable." Yogacharya Mother Hamilton followed in the footsteps of these great masters.

After Yogananda left the body in 1952, Mother Hamilton received inner direction to go to India where she inwardly knew she would find the support she required to fully go through the "Mystical Crucifixion." There at Anandashram, in Kerala, South India, she placed herself in the capable hands of Swami Ramdas and Mother Krishnabai (affectionately known as Papa and Mataji). During months of inner work, Mother Hamilton went through the deepest and most profound spiritual experiences known to humankind. As part of this inner opening, the New Testament scriptures' inner meanings were revealed to her. She saw that hidden beneath the outward story of Jesus was the evolutionary story of the ascent from the human to the Divine.

David finds his way to this great lineage of teachers.

He says:

> When I came to Mother I was a definitely a diamond in the rough, not even a diamond but more a lump of coal hoping one day to shine with light like a brightly lit

diamond! An inner pain brought me to the path, most unwillingly. And this inner pain kept me on the path when I would have gladly wandered away back into the world.

In his biography David speaks of the testing of his resolve and the testing of his commitment by Mother Hamilton. Not only did she invite David to give a talk to the devotees, she also asked him to speak of his inner experiences. He tells us: "Now I had never spoken to anyone about my deepest inner experiences except to Mother, and now she was asking me to say aloud in front of others my most sacred experiences. Mother had always cautioned against talking to others about spiritual experiences." David realized the reasons not to talk and now the reasons to talk. "Not easy, this," he says.

The testing was for a purpose. Ten years later Mother Hamilton ordained David as a minister. He agreed, thinking, "I can serve, I can serve Mother, serve Truth, be a servant of God and to serve the God that is within all people—that I can do! I found a way to be a minister."

David's inner growth continued as he developed his inner agreement to find the Divine path. He speaks of a time just before he started to write poetry:

In the fall of 1976, I sat in a meditation group when a sudden intensity came in my body. My attention was powerfully drawn to my spine and brain. Then, to my amazement, I felt and inwardly heard a snap at the base of my spine. A powerful surge of energy shot up my spine to the base of the skull, then crossed through the brain to a point in my forehead. Then a tremendous feeling of heat formed at a point on my forehead; my whole attention was nailed to this point. It was very powerful, uncomfortable and awe-inspiring all at the same time. I had heard Mother speak of such experiences on her own way to realization—now I felt blessed to have this experience come to me. This experience lasted for perhaps five or ten minutes before it began to subside (time is very difficult to measure in such cases). This was the beginning of an inner transformation that was to last for many years.

With his inward journey progressing, David accepted an increasingly large ministerial role, while Mother Hamilton's health challenges increased as did her resolve to serve God to her last breath. Serving to support Mother Hamilton came at the same time as full-time school and full-time work and full-time sadhana. Mother, in planning for the continuation of the Guru-disciple lineage, told David that she was going to make him Yogacharya (teacher or master of yoga) and that she would be passing her spiritual mantle on to him.

David shares:
> This gift " . . . came as a deep Mystery, with inner potency and meaning that continues to unveil itself to me through the passing years. Far from feeling I deserved such an accolade, I felt deeply humbled and prayed that I would acquit myself to whatever capacity God would give me." David also says, " . . .I, to the best of my ability, put my shoulder to the wheel of this great Work begun so long ago."

On January 31, 1991 Yogacharya Mother Mildred Hamilton entered Mahasamadhi, a yogi's conscious exit from her body. David knew that Mother Hamilton was now in her light body. At this time David says his task was " . . . to find her in her universal Presence beyond the physical realm." And that decision plus other life decisions led David to what he calls the dark night of the soul, that started in 1992.

> At this time I took a leave from ministerial duties as I felt I was in no condition to help others; for, I was entering a dark night of the soul. Mother described this dark night coming at a time when the aspirant has almost continuous communion with God, then all sense of connection disappears. This was my case, and it was to last for two years. Meanwhile I was working fulltime, going to school fulltime, working part-time in an internship, and experiencing a deep emptiness inside that had no solution, but to go on.
>
> Never did I doubt God or the path I was on; what I keenly knew were my own errors, all the ways I lacked the spiritual qualities I knew that I should have, and

most of all how familiar God had been to me before, and now with the curtain drawn, how helpless I felt to get that inner Presence back. There was no joy for me and I struggled just to get through the day.

Time passed:

One night I had a vision. I was walking along a path in the desert. This desert was so beautiful, green and lush with flowers like springtime. The path I walked on was spongy-feeling and the air smelled delicious. I felt God. Oh, it had been so long! Like parched ground receiving fresh water I soaked up the feeling of God. As I looked behind me, from where I had come, the land was charred black, the ground hard, cracked and broken from earthquakes, the air black with soot; I knew the dark, ugly landscape I looked upon was a true representation of what I had been experiencing. When I saw it I let out a cry of anguish of all that I had been holding in for so long! A prayer came, Oh Lord of the Infinite, I have missed you so much. Please never leave me again.

For the next six months I gradually emerged from the darkened gloom into a new Light. I had completed my master's degree and went on to a work in my chosen field, which was very satisfying. One day I received a call from some Kriyabans in Canada who were asking me to help clarify their Kriya practice, then an invitation to come and speak; there were many thirsty souls awaiting my visit. For so long I had felt I was the last one to help others; now the Light came to me at the same time as the expressed need of others. God's ways are perfect and mysterious!

This was in 1995 and yes, David answered the 'call' to engage in his ministry in a new way. And Canadians got to hear Kriya teachings. By 1997 David was increasingly sensing that his inner direction was to engage in work as a full-time minister. While not knowing what would come next, he gave up a position he loved and turned this new phase of his life over to God's design. And, just at that moment Peter Schultz offered to build a tiny apartment for David. He now had a home. Then in 1998, Phyllis Victory, a long-time devotee of Mother Hamilton, sponsored him on a pilgrimage to India. Of course, one very important destination was Anandashram and Swami Satchidananda who was now the god-man guardian of Anandashram. There David found Swamiji "an indispensable help in my realization."

Returning to America, David led a busy life teaching, holding retreats and meeting with devotees in many cities in both the USA and Canada. He says:

> On my return to America I continued a busy schedule of travel to work with various aspirants. Now, and after many years of fully scheduled days, I had time to simply go with the powerful stream up my spine into higher realms of consciousness. No longer was I daily crucified on the cross of vertically upward spiritual power meeting the horizontal daily demands of worldly activity. I was now free to sail into the mystical sea of consciousness without limit.
>
> One day, out of my mouth came the idea that I should spend a year in silence and solitude; again it was an unsolicited idea that came unbidden from some unknown depth. Never before had I considered such an idea; I don't even think I had spent even a day in silence except when there were no others about. I found the perfect place to spend the year: Cloud Mountain Retreat Center. From September 9, 2000 to September 9, 2001, I was in silence and seclusion. During this time of silence I became established in an inner state of stillness that has never left me.

And then another life surprise:

> Toward the end of my year of solitude an inner direction came to me that was yet another surprise. The inner direction was for me to marry Carla, a devoted aspirant who had given sincere service for the

last several years to the Work. I realized that this was an important decision, one I did not take lightly as it affected many people, even the Work itself.

In his journal, David speaks of the levels of reflection and inner and outer affirmation he sought on whether this was indeed the right direction for his life. He received affirmations from all he spoke to and on December 15, 2001, Reverend Larry Koler married David and Carla in a marriage ceremony that came from Mother Hamilton and was based on a ceremony Master created. In early 2002 David and Carla left on a pilgrimage to India. Again, we have poems from this time and much more detail in journals. David and Carla made pilgrimages to India in 2002, 2005, 2007 and 2013. In between these times and ongoing into 2018, David and Carla traveled to different Centers. David says:

> Through this Master lineage, He has freely given the very highest means for making that journey of realization. God and the Masters have decreed this Work out of love and compassion for those who desire nothing less than the highest realization. Far too often we are unmindful of the underlying Reality that gives real peace, joy and wisdom for all; no matter a person's circumstance. Jesus and Babaji are the headwaters of this Work, Lahiri Mahasaya, Sri Yukteswar, Master and Mother bless it, and it will shine in this world as long as there are sincere seekers who desire spiritual transformation.

David closes his autobiography in 2007 with the words:
> This spiritual evolution is the greatest hope for a strained world that is too often filled with conflict, intolerance and separation. Only through individuals gaining their realization of this spiritual Reality will this world come to know its full glory of the Light of the Infinite Divine. May we all put our shoulders to the wheel of this great Work: the upliftment and spiritual evolution of the individual soul and of this beautifully created world.

The Cross and The Lotus web site has many of David's other writings and blog articles where he shares his teachings right up to his Mahasamadhi (August 12, 2019.) As time progresses, David's journals will also be transcribed and placed in publications, along with his more than one thousand talks.

David's last five years were busy and dedicated during the time he was addressing serious health challenges. Always at each step David was fully supported and cared for in complete dedicated devotion by Carla. Carla's sharing at David's Mahasamadhi Memorial Service is included here in *Chapter Eight*.

David always sought for something more in his life. As a young man he deeply sensed that there was more to existence than narrow materialism and superficial personality satisfactions. He sought answers, and he found a teacher and teachings that nurtured an evolutionary process to realization that neverendingly brought him surprises and new heights.

David's poems, approximately three hundred, interweave from start to finish a process that spirals from great height and promise, then spiral down to the valleys to gather up the lost pieces of shame, or blame or shadow, carrying these wounds lovingly up to the transformative heights. It is a climb of a sacred mountain, and with mountains, there are steep climbs, easy paths, valleys, rivers to ford, and false peak after false peak, until the grand top is reached. This is the sacred mountain, unique for us—present for us all. David gloriously shares his fierce determined and joyous living journey up the mountain.

He inwardly sought more meaning. He was called, he responded. In the first set of poems in *Chapter One* we walk with David as he speaks to *The Call* and provides his *Response*. Once his conscious consent to the spiritual process was acknowledged—for consent is the law—David enters the purification process. Tests, more tests, and torturous challenges take him from a superficial ego personality-desire world into his deepest pain. Shadow and light are hinted at in *Chapter Two, The Path of Purification*. His willingness to grow builds a healthy ego, one that can discern clearly. He starts to more deeply, completely and consciously serve a higher calling, a higher Light and Divinity inside—this process he shares with us in *Chapter Three, The Path of Conscious Witnessing*. He becomes clearer, a more refined and conscious discerning instrument for the Divine truth. As this interweaves in his life and inner nature, he claims *Homecoming* with poems in *Chapter Four*. Now he is in a conscious illumined state living in the world and in the light of Divine guidance. Throughout all this time he opens his heart and prays for higher illumined support, and *Chapter Five* features some of those selected prayers. David pays tribute to his Guru-lineage and to other great teachers that influenced him. He honors their Mahasamadhi and the teachings they have left for all humanity in *Chapter Six*. India had so many gifts for David, the life, the teachings, the sacred, and the scenery there impacted him profoundly. *Chapter Seven* brings us *India's Gifts* where David shares his delight. In *Chapter Eight* we honor Mahasamadhi, the dropping of the body, the transcendence to the light body. Over time, David wrote aphorisms, affirmations and principles for living, these have been compiled in *Chapter Nine*. With *Chapter Ten* we find closure for now with David's poignant sharing of a life process, a spiritual evolutionary process that is reachable for us all: We just need to say Yes!

Yogacharya David and Carla, Victoria, B.C. 2004.

Yogacharya David, Sarnath, N. India. 1998.

Yogacharya David, inside Babaji's Cave, N. India. 2005.

CHAPTER ONE
THE CALL AND THE RESPONSE

Can we ever predict when the sacred mountain will appear? Or even that it exists for us? Do we at some deep subtle Dharma level say Yes, even as we are born? There are so many more such questions!

For David, a synchronistic meeting with a friend led to an invitation to attend a talk by Yogacharya Mildred Hamilton (called Mother Hamilton) in 1974. David had found his Guru. Mother Hamilton was ordained by Paramhansa Yogananda of the Kriya lineage. Much later Mother Hamilton ordained David as a minister and later, before she left her body, she designated David Yogacharya to carry the Kriya mantle forward. Now, the path to the sacred mountain truly unveiled. A renewed, serious, dedicated climb began with its relentless, perilous, and blissful guidance.

The Call came at an unexpected time, but in his deep heart, David was ready. He speaks of an aspect of the climb in *My Spiritual India*: "Proceeding through the successive planes of consciousness, what is thought by the world as evolution, is the gradual awakening of the soul to its own complete sense of itself—something, that in truth, it has never ceased to be." He goes on to say, " . . . in truth the soul reclaims its conscious awareness of what it has always truly been."

In *The Call* theme David's poems show us in myriad ways how he received the call to return to soul-consciousness: Infinite Awareness. The Call comes to David from himself, from Mother Hamilton, and from the Divine.

In *The Response* David's poem *Devotee Test: There is a Mountain to Climb* affirms: "The separate 'I' in me gives itself to the great 'I' in You . . . let me be Thy instrument." Here we begin to see David's dialogue with the Divine and his gathering of resources for a climb he now knows will be relentless. In another poem, he calls on the *Master Engraver* to aid and to carve. David says, "Lift me up the mountain . . . put Thy stamp on me forever more . . . protect me in the depths." The depths do come as he follows the path to purification—here David provides us with hints of the steep and perilous journey, and while seriously tempted to abandon the climb, he never gives up.

He understands the temptation, "There are those in the valley who look up to the mountain top, 'It is not so high,' they explain, or 'It is much too high' they sigh . . . Some climb to the foothills and say 'Tis far enough' and return to the valley to tell of their brief experience. Others climb quite far and then say 'Enough for this life.'"

Then, he continues, "Those few, those worthy ones set out over bleak snows, negotiate vast crevices, suffer whatever comes. False peak after false peak with steadfast steps they take, not being overjoyed or over-sorrowed at each new victory or defeat. Until through death's jaws to mountain top they come." He aimed to travel "ever closer to the sun." Through *The Call and The Response* we start on the journey with David.

Poems gathered together in *The Call and the Response* speak to the call as David perceived and received it and share the varying ways in which he internalized his response.

Yogacharya David with Trees in Flower. Washington State. 1990.

THE CALL

You Have Asked Me to Teach

Oh my Divine Mother
You have asked me to teach
As a Seva (service) to You
Whatever good is done
Whatever Light is shared
Whatever Love is awakened
Is a result of Your Grace.
May this instrument
Be ever responsive to Your promptings.
May Your Grace
Ever shine through this work.

Hide and Seek: Be Gracious Now

O Lord
I do not like your game of hide and seek
Come now into Thy child's lonely heart
Make Your Self known
And the sun to shine upon this little one.
Be no miser of Spirit
But gracious evermore,
O Lord, I do not like this game
Come to me now!

Devotee's Test: There is a Mountain to Climb

A test of a true devotee
Does God pervade every thought, feeling and action?
Does the sweetness of God fill their being
So they serve God in all whom they meet?

Such are the tests of a true devotee
And no one outward action may
Indicate their wondrous attainment
For it takes a knowing one to recognize a kindred Spirit.

There are those in the valley
Who look to the mountain top,
"It is not so high" they explain
Or "It is much too high" they sigh.

Some are inspired to look upon the hill
Some are inspired to write about it
Some bow down and worship it
And some gain a burning need to climb.

Some climb to the foothills
And say, "Tis far enough"
And return to the valley to
Tell all of their brief experience.

Some continue on climbing higher still
Till at last they break the tree line
And with that mighty view they exclaim
We clearly see yonder valley and Mountain top.

And with that view they suffice
Their longing for the great beyond,
Risen high, they rest,
"Enough for this life" they think to themselves.

But a few, a hardy few
Dare not rest, cannot rest
Rather they feel impelled to continue
"To the top or die" they affirm gravely.

Leaving behind all kith and kin,
And thoughts of returning with glory,
Knowing they sacrifice all
That humans covet and seek.

Those few, those worthy ones
Set out over bleak snows
Negotiate vast crevices
Suffer whatever comes.

False peak after false peak
With steadfast steps they take
Not being overjoyed or over-sorrowed
At each new victory or defeat.

Pushed past all endurance
With faith they stand fast
Despair does not overcome
And with carelessness they spend their very selves.

Much do they learn
In order to skillfully climb,
Using markers of past travelers
They validate their wandering path.

Onward and upward
The brave juggernaut explore
Knowing no end or beginning
Only endless tracks of white.

Until at last by grace and skill
Through death's jaws
To mountain top they come
And with clear broadening view
They emerge into their own infinite vast space.

Not the same as when begun
Yet strikingly similar are they,
Wisdom's eye sees more than mortal
And stillness belies their activity.

Who can say in words what such a one knows?
Who could convey the changes that journey wrought?
How could those on valley floor
Know what it is to be That?

Spiritual climbers be such as we
With ice pick of faith
And cleats of meditative mind,
We journey from valley to peak
Never a thought of looking back or giving up.

And what is the test of one reaching
That empyrean peak?
That God pervades every fiber
Of thought, feeling and action,
Sweetness of God overflowing their cups
And they love and serve God in one and all.

So come my hardy climbers
Come one and all
Scale those hidden peaks
And call answer to the Enchanters.

Sweet Misery, You are My Friend

Emotions arise from the fallen past;
Sensations strike devastating blows.
My mind merges in the murky water,
Slowly it begins to sink lower.
O sweet misery, you are my friend.

An imaginary lover gains access to my mind,
She greedily absorbs me all in all.
I recognize the unpleasant odor of a lie,
I see her for the misery she is.
All is in vain, and vain is in all.

My much-tested mind comes back within,
Too many times I have followed that wearisome trail.
It leads but unto darkness,
A hell that is dark and bottomless.

Upon the sanctuary of my deep re-remembering
Do I re-emerge
Foreseeing the nights of calamity's woe,
I reawaken to the Enuberance to whom I belong.
Thin lightning shafts begin to dawn,
Morning birds of heaven and peace do again ascend.

O sweet haven of heart and mind,
Lovely and precious is your gift to me.
Dark and meaningless is the world below.
Luminous and wise is the greatness above.
Oneness above and below, to the left and right.
Home, Home once again.

Awaken Me O Divine Mother

In Purity You have called me to Yourself
But also in lurid outer forms
You come to tempt me away.

You are the sacred Power within
And You secretly yearn to rise,
To awaken divine experience Itself
Through subtle channels that flow.

But age-old patterns divert
That steady minded approach
And seek to divert that power to lesser gods
In vain pursuit of happiness.

Awaken in me O Divine Mother
Pure love for thy Divine Form alone.
Burn those puny gods in sacred flame
And free me now and always, in Thee alone!

My Hari is Near

Love pervades night and day
Where is my Hari not?
O who can hear his flute's call?
Who knows his love, his very nature?

Love abounds in heart and soul
Sweetness permeates the air I breathe
The body is slain in love's embrace
And soul melts in its rapturous time.

O my Hari is near
He calls the name of names,
His flute soothes the animal nature
And guides it home.

And look, what is that?
Under starry canopy goes on to dance
Krishna and his gopi lovers
Moving in sweet ecstasy's embrace.

O Krishna my love
Make of me an eternal lover
Like blessed gopis of yore
Eternally fixed on Thee alone.

Make me see you in every leaf and branch
Make me know you as the all in all,
Make my spirit blend in yours
Until at last we move as one.

Tell Me My Lads

O sing my lads
Sing a song of joy
And make it speak to me
A song that tells a story blessed.

O sing my lads
Of a time of yore,
When men followed the stars
And kings watched for holiness.

And tell me my boys
Tell me true and clear
Of how a child was born
Under a star of wonder and mystery.

Can you show me a time
When shepherds knew angels
And wicked rulers feared the light
And humble folk grew in holiness?

Yes, tell me my lads
Of those sacred events
When dreams became prophecy
And prophecy made reality.

And most of all my dear ones
Can you make that story live
Live and breathe with heart and soul
A living song sewn deeply marrowed.

For the song I want
The song I need
Is a song that finds a way
Of giving birth to something new in me.

O sing my lads
A story timely and timeless
Of a child pure born of the heart
For everyone on this tiny earth.

For the spirit grows weary
Without renewed covenant,
So sing me a song my lads
A song that makes me new again.

O Lord, My Comfort, Come to Me

O Lord, You are my comfort,
When I hurt, You soothe me,
When empty, You fill me,
When tired, You energize me.
I see You as a presence solidly in me,
I feel You soothing me in every nerve,
I hear You as sweet sounds surrounding me,
I taste You as fulfillment.
O Lord, You are my comfort
Come to me
Make me know You are near and dear
Teach me to experience the fullness of Your presence.
Be it ever so.

Hear the Savior's Call

Midnight glance reveals that night
When the savior struggled with fear,
Mighty was that darkened fight
As forces of heaven and hell drew near.
Blood seeped from forehead pores,
Temptation struck with mighty blows
Soul stooped down to its very core
Blazing Light reduced to tepid coals.

Hanging on during the darkest darkened night
Refusing to let go of Heaven's Voice,
Blinded eyes seeking sacred sight
Knowing truly there is but one choice.

O brothers and sisters hear me now,
Mankind's future hung in peril
On that midnight lonely vigil's prow
When human soul wrestled with its devil.

But devil is but lived spelled backwards
And that darkened night is all about
Setting spiritual hero on the throne heavenward,
Deep seated faith replacing deep seated doubt.

O my friends let this be known
This is all mankind's story
As each one has a darkened night alone
Every soul can awaken to its own Glory.

Each one has a savior deep down
That daily suffers human indignity,
Every day is opportunity to be done
Acts that reflect spiritual integrity.

Every day we are tempted by nature's greed,
Each moment we build or destroy,
Our sacred temple in every deed
When with our free will we do employ.

So, come my brothers and sisters
And hear the savior's call
One who has shown us the way to love without fear,
And resurrect love and life within, and in us all and all.

Divine Search for God

Divine Search
I search for God
The God who is all in all
All time, all space, all matter
Matter and Beyond Matter.

Matter, that translucent
Shimmering Presence
But, bereft of that presence
I searched in vain.

I looked, looked within
But all was black
Without trace of light or uplift
Sometimes, without hope or comfort.

A hard path
Uphill, without respite,
Yet driven
Driven was I to go.

To go within
Seeking, but not sure for what!
Yet seeking
Through inner darkness and misery.

Not spurred by logic, but an inner need
A need that would not go away
A need that would not be subverted.

This need was an exacting master
Punishing me with inner pain,
Inner yearning,
When ignore it, I would try.

But then! Suddenly
Emerged some hope, some light.
There! And there again, some oasis
Only to be gone again.

Curse this need, this powerful need
Why do I need?
Why cannot I be satisfied, like others
Curse this need.

Again, yet again
Oasis comes more frequently,
Promises of future promises
The need drives on, now with headlights.

Frequency of oasis
Makes dry desert even more dry,
And drive continues to drive,
But now with more frequent respites.

Lo, the goal arises!
Light is more abundant than dark,
Life affirms the driven need
And understanding overreaches darkness.

Now, and now again
I do not curse the need,
Rather, I bless it
Bless its invisible giver.

For it has driven me beyond,
Beyond what I had known
Beyond my comfort,
Beyond my own self-made ignorance.

Now I bless the curse
For it has made me see the Light
Beyond myself
Beyond my own understanding.

And Lo
When I saw,
Saw that which I have searched for,
Saw that Sublime Light.

I was stunned, dumbfounded,
For what I did not expect,
For what I could not expect,
That Light, was also searching for me!

O Sadhakas

Let us journey home together
For each is born and dies alone
But here we have glad privilege
To walk hand in hand.

And once knowing our joy
And finding it a boundless font
Each drinking deep to their fill and more!
Find even more joy in sharing it with all.

So be glad sadhaks
The journey may be long and difficult
But, it is in the right direction!
And we will live to see thy homecoming.

Feel God's Presence in every Cell

Feel God's presence in every cell,
Lift your eyes upward to the hills.
It is infinite love that you seek,
Don't be shy, don't be meek.

For who is God but our very self,
He's not dull, don't put Him on the back shelf.
Bring Him right out front, in front of your eye,
God is not imagination, not a lie.

Be bold and ask the Infinite for His Grace,
For it is only by God's boon, that we may see His face.

Love thy neighbour as thy self,
Love the Lord, for He is thy self.
Be True to Him forever and always,
Pray that the Love of God will always stay.

Inner Pain Was My Master

Eternal I into this dark cavern
Of earthly existence so alone,
Formed of mud, sense and awareness,
Fused with body, higher knowledge had I none.

Fears, desires, confusion abound,
Thoughts of wanting nothing but to hide,
Or if to be seen, wanting only glory
To be beheld far and wide.

O dear little self
How much you struggled, how much you cried,
O dear little one
How you hoped, how you feared, how you denied.

Denied the fears, denied your deeper hopes.
Yet, within you, beyond your hopes for earthly glory,
You held a dream, half thought, half spoken,
Yet, a dream all the same.

As you aged, entering adulthood,
You thirsted for more than the world showed,
Yearning for a distant Light
Yet, a dream all the same.

For the Light was a belief
With glimmers only here and there.
Inner pain drove you on
O little self, how you did despair.

Inner pain was your master,
Your pilot and plight,

And how you yearned for something new
To be born in the Light.

Finally, with faltering steps,
You found your emissary of Light,
Your very own spiritual Master
To teach you how to take Flight.

Flight into realms of spiritual hue,
Flight beyond this body and structure
Into a broadening view,
Into existence of exquisite lustre.

Rome was not built, no, not built in a day
And neither does the chrysalis
Grow wings and emerge from darkened cave
All at once.

But slowly and unsurely
With steps not in a straight line
That little one grew in Spirit,
A new Consciousness began to refine.

And this transformation has a momentum new,
Shame and ignominy replaced
By love and understanding ways
And ever-new Light it may adore.

And life in that cavern of old
Seems more like a long-lost dream,
Set in my course now
My soul continues in Light that redeems.

O Great Spirit of All

O great Spirit of all,
Bring thy gifts to us.
Give to us, thy children,
Your wondrous works of joy.

Create in us a giving heart,
Tell us of our selves.
O Creator of all, you alone
Are real to the God-man.

Many use your name,
Few know your Word.
How long will we wander from thee?
How long will we suffer cruel duality?

Our wandering eyes keep us
From thee, ever outward do we look for you.
Transform that urge to the
Inner kingdom, there to find, you abide.

THE RESPONSE

O Master Engraver, Lift Me Up The Mountain

O Divine name, take me deeper into God,
Be my guide and savior.
Like a ship keeping me afloat,
Carrying me across the sea of delusion.

Encompass me with Thy Bliss,
Bless me with Thy wisdom.
Fill my lamp with oil,
And light it for me also.

Lift me up the mountain,
Carry me to the Christ.
Long in meditation do I wait,
For Thy Voice, which art the Rock of Ages.

Be Thou a Divine magnet,
Drawing me ever closer to the Sun.
Wilt Thou now come to me,
Wilt Thou now be mine forever.

O Master Engraver
Carve me into Thy Word.
Put Thy Stamp on me forever more,
Thy Image is my Image, Thy Thought my thought.

O Divine Word, carry me to the heights,
Protect me in the depths.
Like an Ark you surround me,
Forever will you keep me afloat.
Om, Peace, Bliss, Amen.

O Lord my Love for You is Incomplete

O Lord, my love for you is incomplete,
Sometimes I love what this body wants
More than I am moved by Your wants
And my desires mean more to me than You,
There are times when fears in me
Override Your Love and Wisdom.

O Lord, please teach me to love You perfectly
Make Your will preeminent in my life
That I might do as a perfectly honed instrument
Responds to a master craftsman,
That I will seek You as my only comforter
And the fulfiller of all my desires,
That out of love for You
I will serve all whom I meet.

O Lord, I sincerely pray
From deep within my soul
That You will grant this petition
And make my love for You perfectly complete.

Just for Today

Just for today
I will trust in You,
Just for today
I feel you close and present,
Just for today
I remain in the moment unafraid.
Om Sri Ram, Jai Ram Jai Jai Ram

O Beautiful One in my Heart

Infinite peace, Infinite Wonder,
Sorrow and pain are plowed asunder.
O beautiful One in my heart,
A fire of devotion in me did you start.

Love has blossomed forth,
Grace has blessed me with its report.
I have escaped my ego-made prison,
And to the heaven of my being,
I make my ascension.

Ecstatic Joy show me the way,
To live in perfection day to day.
Always will I be with you O Lord,
To live without you I cannot afford.

Grace in action I can see you clearly now,
How you remove us from sorrow's plow.
Never leave me Lord, never end,
Never alone do I want to be
Without my Friend.

I Walk Alone, I Walk and Walk

I walk alone in my walk,
I walk alone, I walk and walk.
But do not walk in loneliness,
For I feel your gentle and sweet caress.

I hear you talking to me
In the stillness of my mind,
Your voice is silent, sure and fine.
I feel your presence, I feel you there,
I know you love me, I know you care.

You whisper sweetness to my soul,
Of your wisdom, you let me know.
I taste your pleasure through my earthly senses,
But I am always aware of your greater presence.

I walk alone in my walk,
I walk alone, I walk and walk,
But I don't walk in loneliness,
For I feel you here in your vast fullness.

O Lord Use My Imperfections

O Lord
Use my imperfections for Your perfection,
Take my weaknesses and turn them into Your strength
Transform my indifference to Your passion,
Remember me always
Accept me as I am,
Make use of the material I am
And transmute it to the Glory of
Who You Are.

It is You Lord

It is You Lord
Who has created this universe.
It is You who sustains it
And it is You who withdraws it
Back into Your Being.

It is You O Lord
Who has become every particle of nature,
It is You who stands behind all creation,
And, yes, it is You who manifests as uplifting
Great at all times.

It is You Lord
Who has become me, and all beings,
You made me who I am.
You unmake me and remake me at Your whim.

It is You who makes me ignorant, or wise
And You who makes me large or small,
You make me light or heavy
And You who gives me life or death.

It is You Lord
Who makes me think of one thing
And forget its opposite,
When I think of this world
Then I forget You.

And it is You Lord
You, the all-powerful Being
Who makes me see both the world
And You shining in it and beyond it.

It is You Lord
Whom I surrender myself to,
I acknowledge Your pre-eminence
As the author of my very being.

It is You Lord
Without whom I could not live,
Nor breathe nor have my being,
It is You who comes to me as
My Savior, my sweet Guru
And leads me back to Thee, only Thee.

It is You Lord
Who causes me ignorance,
It is You who lifts me to wisdom,
It is You who makes me strive to find You.

Without You nothing exists
You are a first without a second,
You are one who becomes the many
And then returns to the one.

You are time and space,
Emanating from Your word
Matter whirls within time and space,
All comes from You speaking the Word.

It is You O Gracious Lord
Who sent sweetness into our being,
And it is Your sweet sound
That calls us back to Your Remembrance.

It is You who makes us not see You
Like a mother hiding behind a mask,
The child pulls down the mask
To smilingly reveal the mother.

So do You hide behind the mask of creation,
And Lo! When we seek only You
The mask unveils its creator
And we see it is You, only joyful You.

So what we ask O Lord
What we pray
That when we seek You out
Do not delay.

When we strive
Add Your grace to our striving,
And what we seek
Makes us also find.

It is You O Lord
Who has put that prayer in my heart
So that You may find joy in fulfilling it
Because all is You Lord, only You.

I Am Your Instrument

Oh Lord—I am your instrument
For you see through my eyes
And the world shines in splendor
You are the Light of this world.

And I am Your agent
Your love pours through my heart
Like a vast, endless river
And the world is washed clean in Your love.

You painfully break me
And Your compassion issues forth,
It deconstructs this complex world
And salves the world in loving compassion.

Oh Infinite Self
Solo Creator of island universe
You see your puny human vessel
And fulfill Your boundless purpose.

It is my joy—my greatest joy
To be Your instrument
That you use me as your pen
To write Your story in the Book of Life.

Black Clouds of My Divine Mother

Black clouds were all around
There was no ray of hope in sight
Trudging through darkened woods of despair
It seemed an eternity of broken dreams.

Then of a sudden
With blinding flash of light!
You broke through blackened clouds
And the sun made everything bright.

With a laugh You saw my shock
With a giggle You saw my surprise grow
Then tears streaked my face
In relief of pain, and in joy they flowed.

Who could know Your labile mood?
Who would guess You were just behind the cloud?
Who could see the light was about to burst
Where darkness had been standing all about?

O Divine Mother
You are often painted black
And frightening are Your forms
To the outward glance alone.

But You let me penetrate Your guise
And looking into Your dark-covered heart
I see only beauty and laughter
Forever playing behind a beguiling mask.

O my Divine Mother dear
Do not hide Yourself from my searching heart
Reveal to me Your truer Self
And in eternal love and joy, let us ever wink and nod.

Lonely Feelings in My Heart

Lonely feelings in my heart,
Separation of every part.
Where is happiness now?
Why is everything so foul?

Look to see that perfect person,
Where can I go to relieve this tension?
Other people look so filled,
Where can I go to remove this chill?

Vaguely asking why it's so,
Looking outward to this passing show.
Slowly it begins to dawn on me,
It matters not what I say or do.

I start to move from out to in,
I start to move to the light from the dim.
I fail as I miss the mark,
And I start to move back to the dark.

I try again with great tenderness,
I start to see I've been in quite a mess.
Fulfillment begins to expand,
I know I've hit the mark as I begin to stand.

God rushes in to fill me up,
Jesus comes in for awhile, to sup.
O Blessed Lord I've found you again,
My incessant prayer is to keep me from delusion.

Power Surges

Power surges through the body
Rendering helpless all movement.

How does the vessel not break?
Into countless particles of soul?

Wondrous Divine touch
Shakes to pieces human clinging.

Can body remain after such storms?
Experience says definite yes!

O Benefactor of ageless soul
Be generous and kind in your movements.

Take care not to let go your grip
On this puny servant of yours.

Eight and twenty years
Have you taken residence in this one.

Eight and twenty years
Since the Elephant awakened inside this hut.

You are ever interested in all souls
But especially you are in your seekers.

You are ever moving through all
But especially in your willing instruments.

Be kind and generous O Benefactor
With your servants under submission.

Shower Love and comfort as well as power
Upon those attending upon you.

Spiritual Sleep

When at times we fall in Spiritual Sleep,
When our mind is taken down deep.
O when God refuses our unceasing call,
When our soul takes on unending fall.

Should our tears begin to run,
Always turn toward the Sun.
For Therein lies the secret,
Of why we are in a delusive net.

There lies the secret sorrow,
Why we are shaken to our very marrow,
For when God hides his face,
We cry for mercy in a daze.

Then from our Soul Spring bubbles our Love,
To flood the Heavens up above.
Then returns our Lord to us,
With Smiling face and so robust!

When you have a longing for another person,
You think you belong in another season.
When your heart feels like a chasm,
Your whole being is in a prison.

Have faith in God on High,
For it is in his absence that you sigh.
That empty feeling in your heart,
Is God's path you are about to start.

But if your mind is at a loss,
And says I have no Love for Godliness.
Then get down on your knees and start to pray,
For the Love of God to come and stay.

Say to him way down deep,
I have no Love for you to keep.
I want to love you but I don't feel it,
I have no devotion I must admit.

O Lord give me Love's gossamer wings,
So to your abode I can fly to sing.
And come to you with devotional feeling,
To know True Love with real feeling.

For to Love God is not imagination,
A Saint's Love has greater power than any nation.
God cannot ignore true Love,
And he will descend on you in white Light,
Like a dove.

Your Will

O Lord You know every part of me
O Lord there is no nook or cranny unknown to You,
O Lord take this raw material and build a fit Temple to you.
O Lord make this mind glow with Your arduous Worship.

You are the protector to the humble,
You are strength to the faithful,
You are Bliss to the Yogi,
You are the All in All to the surrendered.

It is You Who have created this child in
Your Image and likeness,
It is You Who has spun this Divine Lila of separation,
It is You Who art the Savior to the wayward,
It is You Who must make the impossible possible.

I do not come as a beggar, someone unknown to You,
I do not seek for something that is not my rightful due.
I do not seek crumbs of paltry answered prayers,
I do not come for anything less than your very Self.

I know this cannot be bartered for as merchants do,
I know this does not come without paying full measure,
I know this does not come with study alone,
I know this does not come by being good alone.

I know the price for Your very self
I do know it is love for You alone
I do know it is surrender of all my self
I do know this is what is required.

I give to You my works,
I give to You my thoughts,
I give to You my love,
I give to You my all in all.

You will give me perfect love for You,
You will give me perfect service to You,
You will create a perfect temple Within,
You will give to me Your very Self!

Through Trials I Grow

Stillness in God I find,
Turns my body into a shrine.
The world tosses me to and fro,
It is through trials that I grow.

Hanging on to the Mother's shirt,
I fly by troubles in a spurt.
Keeping God ever on my mind,
Soon my whole being will shine.

What greater words could I know,
When God Christ Guru through us do flow.
Hang on to God for dear life,
See through all stress and strife.

Trudging ever forward on my path,
Letting God be my rod and my staff.
Flying into his arms with childlike glee,
Be Simple, Happy and Free.

Peace and Stillness are my friends,
Toward the center is my trend.
Joy races up my spine,
In my head it explodes sublime.

O God expand through me,
Thrills run all throughout my tree.
Bliss is my natural home,
Sadness has taken wing and flown.

New kingdoms within do unfold,
Truth that shines remains untold.
O Holiness haloes my being,
The whole world takes on a sheen.

My beloved, hear my words,
Within you is God's Word.
Look into your own heart,
The journey is inward,
Now's the time to start!

Morning Jewel

Waves tossing this boat about
Upon Thy infinite sea
Vacillating rhythms of have and have not
Foreboding thoughts of catastrophe.

Sickened by this constant toss
Between shores of opposites,
Afraid what I have may be lost
And those losses will consume all profits.

"And what profiteth a man
If he gains the whole world and loses his soul?"
What fool would make this bargain
To risk all for a passing show?

That which truly exists
Can never cease to be,
Eternal Light shining through shrouded mists
Constant presence of the Almighty.

And that which is unreal has never been
Though our beliefs tell us it is so,
Passing shadows will oh so darken
Our pure mirrored mind that truly knows.

A room stands darkened
By a thousand years of night
Is in a brief moment illumined
When once it knows the light.

So our darkened mind can know
What it is to see
The Light that casts this shadow
When once the veil loses its property.

Swords of sharpened minds
Prepare for mighty battle
To smite that cord that binds
And tests the soul's true mettle.

Many may fall in that terrible fight
Casualties there will be
Blood and strife will sear that night
As triumphant soul struggles to see.

That first streak of morning Light
That slowly comes to view,
Inspiring heart and mind with sight
Of diamond sparkles caught in morning dew.

Suddenly on distant horizon
Is seen that blazing orb
Dispelling heavy night with mighty sun,
In that Light we are absorbed.

Only then in day's full Light
May we see nights errored thoughts
Revealing a flawless jewel shining bright
Knowing well the price with which it was bought.

Arise, Awake

Arise, Awake!
It may seem early
But who knows?
I may be Late!

Arise, Awake!
Crows a bird aloft
At heaven's sounding horn
Leading us ever home to Pearl's gate.

And, rising, rising, rising,
Past paltry shimmering gold
Finds erstwhile joys of old
Growing stale and putrid.

Look neither left nor right
On thy morning ride
But straight for the sun
Lest ye not wake before fall of night.

Onward, onward!
Cried the prophets since old
But who cares to listen?
"Is it not tiresome to always go forward."

But delay is quicksand!
And tempting as it might seem
Turns winged flight to feet of lead
And sweet-scented dreams to thick mired land.

So, arise, awake!
Be it ever so with you
That you may know the One
And in Bliss forever stay!

Blessed Lord Let Me Be Thy Instrument

Blessed Lord
You who art the Creator of all
The sun the moon and the stars
The spinning earth and galaxies.

You who have set into motion
Vast universe and the atoms,
You who have created me
Down to my tenderest and most
Whimsical thoughts and feelings.

I bow to You. O Lord
The separate I in me
Gives itself to the great I in You
As a token of my trust in You.

Take my life O Lord
Do with it as you will
Let me be an instrument
Of Thy Will.

In *The Call and The Response*, David has committed to travel the sacred mountain path. He has agreed to acknowledge who he really is and untie the knot of ignorance. This knot brings recoil from the spiritual, and hence bewilders the human mind. He enters the path of a seeker for the pure and supreme light and is determined to verify it through direct personal experience. As he enters the path of purification his faith is tested.

Yogacharya David, India. 2005.

Yogacharya David, Cloud Mountain, Washington, USA. 2000.

Chapter Two
The Path of Purification

The Call has been answered, responses abound, now to commit to the climb. This naturally leads to the Path of Purification. David enters this path with the tenacity of a true warrior, an Arjuna as written of in India's most sacred text, *The Bhagavad Gita*.

As David clearly shares, looking at the mountain, admiring the mountain, climbing part way up is of no use. He must commit to climbing to the top, no matter what befalls—to the top it will be!

In *My Spiritual India* David shares intonations of the agony this deep human change of focus takes as the habit and programmed aspects of his being shift to 'Thou Alone.' He speaks:

> Thou Lord, You have wrenched my soul, wrung it out of all worldly moisture. You have made me seek You and have put this pain in my heart. You make me wretched without You, then You lift me up on blissful wings. I reject this transient bliss, for it comes and goes. Not a child am I, to be given a cookie of experience and sent on my way! I am satisfied with nothing less than Your universal vision. Take away your visions, Your divine personalities and blissful experiences. I am not to be trifled with. I will not succumb to anything less than Your absolute and continuous darshan. To see You in all, as All, forever All! . . . I have left all, all that I have ever called my own at Your feet. Take this body, this mind, these emotions and do with them as You will, but, "Free my people!" That is all, that is all I want!
>
> (pg. 270)

This means, as David stresses, that he must find measurable ways to escape his perceptual programming, ways to undo the egoistic knots that hold him 'small.' He must release the personality's torpor and the lower sense desires, the useless rationalizations and prison-minded robot-like victim tapes his small self activates to keep his zeal dampened to low.

David expresses the battle well as he speaks of the dual perspectives, the illusory-band-width life versus a truly awake living connection with his own deep sacred that is aligned to Universal Oneness. He is asking for freedom from enslavement, freedom to greet his eternal Oneness that is uniquely free and divine. The Path of Purification features poems that share a sense of David's climb, as sense of how wretched he could be, and his sheer determination to go the full route up the mountain.

As Reverend Larry Koler reported at David's memorial, in 2014 David wrote:

> I will tell you something you already know, something about me, but words can never quite tell it all. Each day is a crucifixion for me. The crown of thorns of pain and heat continues unabated down through these many years. And when I focus too much of the mind on certain things, then the heat and pain get turned up. I have learned that this is not something I can muscle my way through and get to the other side; the heat and pain has never been amenable to that. On the other hand, there are other things that this inner Force and Intelligence allows me to do easily. So, I may be able to read a novel but not a spiritual book. Other times I will read only a spiritual book and not novels. I can go to Seattle for Service, but as soon as we turn into the driveway here the crown of thorns is activated. There are times when I can watch a movie, other times I need to be in silence and seclusion. It has been interesting, I feel God and Gurus' footprints all over it, but it does limit what I can do, for how long I can do it and when. What I am allowed to do, and what I personally would like to do is often so very different. However, feeling that it is God who works through me in this strange way, I surrender to what God within wills.
>
> I write all of this by way of saying I do not know what God will allow me to do, for how long, or when, but I know what I feel prompted to have happen for

Mother and for the Work. His will does reign supreme, and I know whatever He does through this form and others will be exactly right for the situation and we will fulfill what Mother has given us to do.

Reverend Larry tells us David paid a continuous price for his state of consciousness:

> Rereading this gives me intense pain and sorrow for him and all he did for us and for God's work. Mother prepared him for many years and she gave her mantle and even her title to him. I know that she did this for a good reason—so that he would not have others gainsay him and to give him full confidence in the work he was to do for her. But, recently I have thought that this was a great burden for him to carry. All of her work was left in one person's hands and that person had to be strong enough to handle it. Mother had, it seems, unending confidence in her choice. He has proven her right. He has completed his life in perfection and as a perfect example for us all to follow. When God calls we must all answer the call and carry out the task set for us. God is indeed great!

Tears are Running Down my Cheek

Tears are running down my cheek,
My heart rips in two as I try to speak.
Sorrow clutches at my heart,
I feel separated from the start.

I really hurt deep down inside,
I want to run but I cannot hide.
My stomach tightens as tears flow,
My whole body trembles at the mighty blow.

I call to the Friend of friends when in need,
I grasp for Him in desperate greed.
I struggle to find His hidden Word,
I look to see Him, lurking behind the absurd.

O how my heart rends for Thee,
Through my tears I begin to see,
Then you recede once again,
And disappear back into the dim.

I call on You in greater faith now,
I am your child, you'll heal me somehow.
You can't resist my unceasing call,
I know you'll catch me at the end of my fall.

Warm Love begins to trickle in,
I can't help but have a little grin.
O Lord I love you so,
You are my Life, my Love, my Soul.

It is You Alone

Thy loving Touch
O Lord
Heat and cold
Pleasure and pain
Ups and downs
Are but the loving caress
Of Your blessed Hand.

In what private intimacy
You give that sacred touch
That makes Your Presence known,
What gentle assistance it is
That it is Your stroke in good and bad.

In all my life, my Beloved
You make Love to your devotee,
In all experiences
It is only Your life
That runs through my veins.

The body wants to say
"This is good, this is bad."
"I like this, I hate that."
But the Supreme Intelligence
Knows but One Life.

O blessed One
Teach this mind, again and again,
Not to judge as the world judges
Rather, illumine this mind to know that all touches are Yours.

And Yours is not a cruel hand
Not thoughtless or unmindful
But every touch, carefully measured
With a loving attention
A careful repose.

You take away
You add
You increase ten-fold
You empty the cup clean
All by Your perfect Will.

Fill me, O Master of All
Fill me with Your Light
So that every pleasure and pain
Every heat and cold
Are known to be Your loving caress.

Then, and then alone
Will separation be dead
And love supreme will Live!
In everyone, everything,
At all times, in all places,
It is You alone.

You, my dearest lover
You meet me in the darkest night
You blind me and make me cry out,
All this you do
So to release me once and for all
Of all my loathsome fear.

O my Kali Mother
Take my head
Hang it on Your body
And set me free in Thee
Forever in Thy Bliss!

Misery—Get Behind Me You have No Power

O misery, you terrible miser,
Get behind me, you have no power.
Freedom in God, the great Ones have taught,
Love and wisdom springs from every thought.

Let Christ be your mate throughout your life,
And send the devil to its endless plight.
No evil has power over me,
Past all duality do I see.

Proclaim the message proud and clear,
This is 'Your Life' and you have no fear.
For to see God as all in all,
Is sure knowledge you will not fall.

Rise up from your dream state,
And see Oneness with God as your fate.
Delay no longer in this worldly cycle,
Maya has no power in the spiritual.

May Love and wisdom be your two children,
And see God hiding behind all of creation.
For when you see any division,
You do not see with God's vision.

Tears

Tears
Tears of repentance
Tears of joy
Tears flow.

Who can say what is the cause?
Only love of God can be
The reason for such tears
Only His forgiveness can explain.

I let go
I let go of all trespasses against me
I let go
I let go of all past hurts and pains.

Tears flow
Shivers up my spine
Hair stands on end
Earthquakes cleanse.

Please forgive
Please forgive my trespasses
All those times I have sinned
Sinned against God and man.

O Lord
Lord, I am weak
Lord, I have no discipline
Lord, I have fallen short.

O Lord
It is You
Your grace alone is sufficient
Sufficient to uplift and purify me.

I am leveled
Leveled to the ground
Only You can animate me
Only You can make me live.

I await my Dear One
I await Thy Presence
I await Thy call
I await.

Tears dry
I am empty
I am an empty vessel awaiting You
Empty.

Peace
Peaceful and cleansed
You come in such a gentle way,
Gentle, intimate friend and Presence.

O Lord, I live
I live only for You
I surrender myself to You
Tears, forgiveness, surrender and joy.

Walking the Razor's Edge

Behold my Divine Mother,
Radiance, Wisdom and Love itself.
Like a light in the dark,
Bringing music to the deaf and
Color to the blind.

Here we are limping, trying to walk
The razor's edge,
Behold the Mother Divine beckoning us ever on.
How we struggle ever onward,
There She stands, like a Mother beckoning
Her child's first steps.

Often we fall, sometimes very hard,
As we recover in sorrow and shame,
We look up to our Mother's Omnipotent Love.
She comes to us in such humility,
With her bewitching smile,
She changes us never to be the same.

As the master gardener, She waters us with love,
She weeds us of our fruitless branches
O Divine Mother, shine on us like
The sun to the tree,
Create in us the Son of God
You so clearly see.

Behold my Divine Mother,
Radiance, Wisdom and Love itself.
Like a light in the dark,
Bringing music to the deaf,
And color to the blind.

SADHANA

O my Beloved
My Infinite Beloved
Trials tear my skin
Darkness enshrouds me
I quake at the ferocity
I am forced to a state at their perversions.

I stand against the tide
It pulls strongly at me,
I sternly remind myself of who I am
A terrible battle is on
And I fight for my Life
I slide toward the abyss
Fascinated and repelled simultaneously.

Against all odds I creep to the Light
The black hole continues to grip still
I seek my refuge and purge the awful beast,
Again and again I look to the Light
The battle seems neverending, overwhelming
Then, Lo! A break, I step into the Light
I bow in deep gratitude to the Lord of Light, blessings.

Now I stand free, strong
I sing my praise
How darkness derives its power? Who can say?
But one thing is sure and proven
Light abides, preserves for good
And destroys the dark
And restores the soul once again.

Destruction's End

The alternating world
Passes through my middle
Agony to Ecstasy
And back again.

I feel oneness
With all humanity
Yet I stand alone
Under uncomprehending gaze.

The world cracks and crumbles,
Titanic cataclysms,
Tortured twisted forms
Cry out and then are gone.

Unconscious nature and Man
Are feast for
The Destroyer's yawning jaws
All go tumbling in.

The Cosmic Play
Continues inside of me.
I witness these forces vast
And shake with their power.

As witness I feel the screams
Of destructive sounds
And sirens of pain
Reverberating throughout my cells.

I Am the Witness
Of this stupendous play
It all happens inside
Of me.

I cannot move
One microscopic inch
From where I see
All this happening.

I cannot flinch
In shock or horror
Or identify
With passing scene.

My insides twist and tremble,
Earthquakes clash and groan,
A thousand voices cry out
And then are gone.

Day after day
Apocalypse continues its course
The Destroyer sweeps all away
Leaving only the Witness.

In sudden stillness
All comes to a stop
Peace is known
The shadow loses power and drops.

The grinding motion
Begins again,
The Destroyer
Is grinding His teeth once more.

And so it goes
Without respite,
All the while
The Witness smiles.

Anger's Quest

Anger's quest is for mastery
Yet anger does not possess the wisdom required,
Anger is blind, deaf and anything but dumb
Anger is fire spreading uncontrollably.

All this is anger orphaned
When anger is united to its rightful parent
It is a force that prevails over inertia and even evil itself.
Self's wisdom is father, love is mother to anger.

Reunite family of wisdom, love and anger
Become a force for the good and upliftment,
Orphaned it is a wreck
United it is good and strong.

Feel within this union,
See in the mind's eye its actions,
Experience the force tempered
Making love's wisdom ever in the fore.

Dark Ghosts become Angels of Light

In the beginning my quest was an
Inarticulate urge towards going beyond
The pain I found myself in.
As time proceeded in my quest
I found the goal became clear.
Now my sweet soul is filled with
The unlimited Goal of my search.

Pain has turned to joy!
Blindness dropped its blinders and revealed
A Divine Vision!
Graves of yesterday's disorders opened
And dark ghosts have risen into
Angels of Light.

Assailed by Delusion's Plight

Assailed by delusion's plight
Laughing with devilish delight.
Hark! here comes Anger's storm
Soul's purity is raped and torn.

The onslaught of anxiety,
Now the attacks of cruelty,
Watch out for that cannon ball
Coming from the tongue with all.

Nervousness is trembling so
Foulness of mind is rising for the death blow,
Love and light have all fled
God and kindness are dead.

The warrior of light lifts his mighty bow
With strained will he staggers low
With mighty will summons within
He yells God, Christ, Guru
With will enough to win.

Stand Valiant

Be a savior for God!
Love's champion and His star.
Dark Knights storm your fortress,
Stand valiant, you are strong.

Your colors are gold, blue and white,
You stand handsome and strong.
It is God's soul, mind and body you have.
Stand valiant, you are strong.

Victory is yours O warrior,
With each defeat you grow stronger.
You may lose a battle, but the war is yours.
Stand valiant, you are strong.

O Son of God,
Know who gives you your strength.
He has unlimited power,
Stand valiant, you are strong.

People storming at you left and right,
Peace is retreating out of sight.
Frustration runs your mind every which way,
It's beginning to look like a dark day.

Hold on, God will save the day,
Joy will return to stay.
Hold that image perfect in your mind.
Return insults with silence,
And harshness with kind.

Show your best to your enemy,
Soon they will begin to see.
As sunshine affects the morning flower,
So will your Being begin to tower.

To the wicked say not a word,
Your peace will spread, be assured.
As God within begins to shine,
That peace, they will want to find.

God is all in all,
All things will awaken to this call.
Men are always perfect in spirit,
Be ever sure to keep your Real Light.

O Humility

O Brother humility
Open my eyes that I may see.
Notions of pride and wit are naught,
But enemies to be fought.

Humility, bless me with thy sight,
So that I might see God's greater might.
Small do we stand in comparison,
When we look upon the sun.

What can you do that has not been done?
Is there anything new under the sun?
Knowledge and power come from a greater source,
Could you change the Earth's course?

If you have any pride at all
Let it be dedicated to God's call.
Always remember who's the real doer,
The Lord is the only Mover.

Be the dust on a great Saint's feet,
Never a hollow reed, with no meat.
O Lord grant us this prayer,
Bless us with humility as our profit's share.

Faith Out of Sight

O faith out of sight,
When storms shriek throughout the night.
Fear clutches at my heart,
Pulse rate goes off the chart!

Anxious looks from here to there,
Pressure almost too hard to bear.
Anxiety is at its height,
Negative feelings show their tremendous might.

A thought slowly begins to dawn,
Fear fades and then is gone.
A knowing faith is in the lead,
Like a champion thoroughbred steed.

Stand up straight, you know
Your real Self is in control.
God is in control of all the parts,
He knows your situation from the start.

You're his son, he loves you so
He will tell you all you should know
See Him protect you through and through
See yourself surrounded by
Gold, White and Blue.

There's no need for
Fear in this worldly drama,
Always connect your thoughts to Rama.
Have faith in God anew,
Know my testimony to be true.

Darkness

The Dark One seems to slip into my dreams
It whispers my helplessness,
The weakness within responds
And gives willing consent.

Delusion spells its web of night,
Its power captures my awareness
Almost complete is its frightening victory
And yet, somehow not complete.

A glimmer shines in that gloom
Something hangs on to sanity's thread,
O but to capture songs of Spring once again
And know sweet happiness as my condition.

Why does darkness seem stronger?
And why do I fight against its tide?
Where does strength derive its endurance?
Can I once again know my good?

I fight against the darkened gloom
I dimly recall past prophets' exhortations
To make valiant the fight for Light
To give my all until my last.

With all might I step towards unseen Light
Without feeling I reach out for Its Presence
Never will I let go, Never give in!
Never succumb, never, never, never give up!

I do not know the Light
I do not know the end
But this I know, this I know,
I will never give up. I will never give up!

There is no Point in Being Sad

Where is thy satisfaction,
Where is it in thy notion.
Do you expect to find happiness here,
Is your perception supposed to be clear?

Wherein does it lie,
Could childish things bring it by.
Would science and knowledge speak
The Truth that we all seek?

Is love of wife, husband and family it?
Maybe a lover or two is the healing kit.
But maybe drugs and drink is where it's at,
We always seem to end up flat.

If the astral plane and mental telepathy,
Is what some say makes us free,
College Profs and intelligence keen,
Is a way for some to get clean.

Listening to a friend is a start,
But soon you see they aren't that smart.
Look and look and still we do not see,
Just exactly how to get free.

But then a Master, someone who knows,
Shows you just what way to grow.
How you meet one is not yet clear,
But once you are there you need not fear.

For in a true Master's hand you will be,
Put through the experiences to set you free.
And though you think you are as great as the sun,
Until you see God you will not know satisfaction.

How else do you explain this show,
Unless you admit you do not know.
But there are a few who seemed to have found,
The Source of all that That makes us sound.

And every one of them testifies to Its greatness and good,
And that we could be better people if we only would.
They say follow me, I have found the way,
To the Dawn of a much finer day.

For although Man is out of harmony,
He still has the possibility to really see.
Man's free will is the difference,
Between harmony or ignorance.

Contact that Peace Divine,
It is that place for which all people pine.
It is that feeling in the heart,
That is the 'Kingdom of Heaven' mark.

If you are restless and have nervousness,
Then seek to have The Christ's caress.
For it is when we go deep down inside,
That we can find God, to whom we can confide.

And when He hears our heartfelt wish,
He grants us what we need, but not a fetish.
For not everything we want is what we need,
There is no room in this Kingdom for greed.

So lift up your heart and make it glad,
There is no profit in being sad.
Never have sorrow, shame or fear,
God's Love is always near.

Be a Slave of the Senses no Longer

Be a slave of the senses no longer,
Being Christ's friend you are stronger
Lift up your lanterns bright,
So that all may see your shining light.

God is strength, power and wisdom,
Residing in Him you break free
Of your man-made prison.
Loud words and empty talk,
Are barriers on your pathless walk.

Wake up your spiritual forces,
March humbly through all your courses.
Many are the pathways that lead to our goal,
But narrow is the gateway
Through which we may bow.

So take God's name everywhere you go,
And he will teach you everything you should know.
And feel sure it's knowledge of His life that you seek
And always feel Him way down deep.

Cast Off Your Mask of Duality

I am the spark of light,
Part of that one great lightning flash.
Together we make up the vast infinity.

O come and let thy love shine,
Be thou a beacon unto the dark ones.
Together we make up the Unlimited One.

Know Yourself to be the Light of the World,
And give yourself gladly to your brother.
Together we make up the all in all.

Lift up your lanterns bright,
Glow with the presence of the Holy One.

Look into your Heart of your heart,
And know this is where the Lord resides.
Together we make up the vast choir of Love.

See God in yourself, the Self of the self,
God will then be seen everywhere, omnipresent.
Together we make up the Ocean of Purity.

Vain people know not this joy,
So cast off your mask of duality.
Together we make up the I am that I am.

Don't Let my Mind go Astray

Take away this material thought,
Don't let my mind go so far astray.
The warrior wins the battle, so hard fought.
Don't let the best worldly thoughts betray.

Come out of your mental caves dim,
Into the sunshine bright.
Don't worry over your long-lost kin,
Step out into the Light.

The Kingdom of Heaven is within,
So do not look without.
Christ will return to reign
That is said without a doubt.

Hell is the seat of our anti-Christ thought,
Longing for senses is his power.
The devil, for worldly things can be bought.
Let us not build a false tower.

God is all things great and good,
He is part and parcel of everything.
Things run on like they should,
All marching towards that great being.

Transform your Urges, Don't Fall

Human love does enjoin,
Limitations stemming from the groin.
Gird yourself and renounce it now,
And go to the Holy One and bow.

Glory exists beyond imagination,
Human love leads only to frustration.
Take on the highest path now,
There is only one path, one Tao.

Seek to elevate all and all,
Transform your urges, don't fall.
Give all your strength purity and reason,
Don't renounce God for any season.

Lift up your life and make it a work of art,
Here is the place, Now is the time to start.
Don't settle for anything less,
Don't stop short while you are still in a mess.

Tears are now running full,
Higher and lower natures begin to pull.
Stand firm in your resolve,
Don't let go now, don't let your standards devolve.

Have faith in God within,
That he has strength to win.
The Lord is Power, Wisdom and Glory,
And that's just the start of this fantastic story!

Sorrow's Center

O verse Divine
I set my hand to thee
O life I reach out to you,
And find it empty.

I hold my heart in my hand,
And find none to receive.
I fall from a great height,
And do not even have the comfort of
Finding a place to crash.

I know not the breadth of my sorrow,
I have not plumbed its depths.
I stand in its center,
And feel its fathomless expanse.

I reached for a friend,
But there was none.
No human could comfort that remorseless plight,
No person could visit me there.

O full blooded Life,
Flood Thy Self on me.
Let me know Thy ebb and flow,
But forget me not.

Sweet agony
I divine thy ways.
I am made empty
So that I might become full.

You have purged me
Threshed me out.
Now fill me
Bring me into Thy Light.

My sorrow is my own
But I share it with humanity.
My pain and joy are entwined
I release my aversion and await
The changing of a season.

O Lord my agony is sweetened by Thy Thought,
You comfort me in my extremity.
Be with me my Lord
And suffer me to be with Thee.

I Did You a Wrong, I Know that Now

I want to ask forgiveness of another person,
To say I'm sorry, that it was a sin.
You think about it, mull it
Over and wonder what to do,
You want to say I'm sorry, you want to be true.

Life can be beautiful and free of sorrow,
But sometimes you hurt other people to their very marrow.
Sorrow grips your heart at its very core,
There seems to be no way out, no opening, no door.

I did you a wrong, I know that now.
And at your holy feet I humbly bow,
Please forgive my trespass against you,
I want to always be your friend, helpful and true.

O Lord How Long Will I Stray?

To my soul search be true
Yet many paths have I wandered afar
Forgetting veritable truths
Until sense drunk, stumbling, have I lost my way.

O how many times
Will I strive and fall short of lofty goal
Falling into worn ruts of old
Finding strength and vision waned?

Forgetful of original thought
Neglectful of things eternal
O how long Lord will I stray
Against my own conscious will?

I pray for my portion of Thee,
My inheritance,
I ask that Thy true nature be revealed
Knower of sublime worlds and beyond.

O Infinite King of sages and saints
Many have striven and fallen short,
Even those who have attained to Thee
Have in previous times tried and failed.

One thing I know for certain
One truth is lodged in my heart,
Beyond all doubt you have smitten me
And I will die in my search for the Beyond.

Body Perfections

O Lord
To teach me to eat properly
To select those foods You have designed
Specifically for this body.

O Lord
You have endowed me with this body
To be an instrument of Your will
Make it perfect—even as thou art perfect.

You have given me free will
And with my free will
I choose to do thy will
In all matters and situations.

So, my dear Friend of friends
Guide my will perfectly
To choose the correct foods
Eat the right amounts at the right time.

Make this body suit Your design
And fill it with Light
Fill it with love and joy
And make it fulfill Your plan.

Make Me Yearn for You

O Lord,
Give me the same love for you
That I have exhibited to others
In fact, make it a love for exceeding all these loves combined.

Give me a love for Your comfort
More than my desire for comfort as a babe
The comfort I sought from my mother
The comfort I needed in body, mind and soul.

Make me seek pleasure in Your Bliss
As I have sought pleasure in the senses
Even as I have felt attractions for things
In the world, let me desire Your Joy
And as I have been repulsed by pain, let
Me abhor separation from You.

O Lord,
As I have consumed so much food with gluttony
Let me hunger and thirst for Your Presence
Be it an unceasing appetite to be with You.

Take all the culmination of my desires in the world
And they have been many
Multiply that by whatever number You will
And make me yearn that much for Thee!

Blessed Lord I Feel Your Presence

Blessed Lord I feel your presence,
You fill me up and accept my repentance.
Lord of Bliss, freedom and vision,
Receive everyone who will sing in unison.

Long are our days that we toil,
We seem to have you, then we recoil.
Will this cycle never end?
Will the law of the world never bend?

Surely it must break and fall,
When the law hears your thunderous call.
Can we do other than call your name?
Will you and I never be the same?

How many times I think I've caught you at last,
Just then troubled thoughts come from the past.
Beauty is all and all,
And yet at times it seems we live in a squall.

Will you end our endless plight?
O when will daylight reach into the night?
Ancient is the promise for freedom,
So does God urge on all of His creation.

Regret Remorse Forlorn

One day I had it in my mind
To cogitate, perseverate, even meditate
On the Infinite
Until I found peace sensate.

So I put myself to work
I sat to quiet my mind
I wanted to concentrate
I wanted bliss sublime.

But what do you know
The first thing to go
Was any sense of order
Any sense of flow.

O my creaky joints
Did so ache
Were those restless ants I felt?
Would that consume my fate?

Now what was that?
What was it I forgot?
O what was that list 'to do'
And yes that other list 'not to do'?

Now where did my mind go?
Into distant past!
O why haven't I done better
Why does time go so fast!

Regret, Remorse, Forlorn
O so many times I've tried and failed
So many times I've fallen short
Upon imperfect dreams I feel dismally impaled.

Now like a rocket ship
Sailing through space and time
My mind travels so quickly
To fantasies in which I'm prime.

O how glorious I could be
Life would be simple, all adoring me
Without care or worry
I could be so perfect effortlessly.

Or would I be imprisoned
Ashamed and so humiliated
With all my faults exposed
Endlessly taunted by ugly crowds, hated.

Now tired of these mind trips
Am I growing now?
Where is my peace?
Why is it so difficult to live here and now?

I settle my mind back
I can feel it a little now
A sense of inner peace
A little joy springing from the loving Tao.

O gentle spirit
Away from gusting thoughts
You came whispering to me
When from restlessness I emerge uncaught.

I see Your bright shining face
And hear Your endless roar
I feel You in my heart
And know you've been with me
And will be evermore.

Only in the restless mind
Could separation ever be
Only in false thoughts of separation
Could the ego think of only me.

Now I'm beginning to know
What saints and sages taught
From every culture and religion
In this one idea they have not fought.

That we are eternally connected
If we only had eyes to see
To one another and the Infinite
And it is ours to know if we could only 'be.'

So let us all throw off this stress and strife,
Commit ourselves to this proposition
And refuse to let ourselves fall
And regress to a dark condition.

In light, love and wisdom
Each one of us have a share
To realize that completeness
And claim our birthright forever more,
If we but dare.

To Now

So another year has gone by,
Your mind reels memories with a sigh,
You look forward to the future bright and clear,
Before you know it, your next birthday is near.

How often we wish to be some other place,
Sometimes our lives seem like a maze,
Then the Light breaks through, and we see clear,
That right now God has always been Here.

This is a poem to Now,
Who, for the last couple of weeks has been on a starve,
The Doc said follow this diet and think thin,
And before you know it you'll be bones and skin.

But today is your birthday,
And now, more cake you say,
If at this crucial time your will fails,
You'll surely break the scales.

God Suffers

God suffers through this body
In pain-heat barely bearable,
Pressure and loving agony
All the world's misery passes through
Sometime lingering—always moving on.

The suffering is not in vain
But it is more-or-less suffering
It brings my world to a stop
And lays waste my human plans.

The suffering is not in vain
But its total purpose may not be known,
It comes in all ways but one,
I do not suffer separation from Him.

I thank Him for that Grace
For that is the one suffering that is unendurable,
And would prove to be my end
For He is my all-in-all, forevermore!

My Sovereign Lord

O Lord, You should govern all my appetites.
All my thoughts should constantly be turned to You.
When I eat, I should eat only in thought of You,
And when I look upon the beauty of nature,
It should only remind me that it is Your Beauty that I see.
At no time should food or carnal appetites make me forget You,
For it is my Gurudev's wish that I should think only of You.
O Lord, I have not the power to change the direction of my mind.
I may try and try, and still fail in the attempt.

However, when You will it so for me, then it must come
to pass!
I humbly submit to You, my sovereign Lord,
You must will it so for me, and for all sincere devotees.
You must see to it that there is never a time for a wandering
mind,
For that is when the trouble starts!
You must cure me of all addictions to this body and the
world,
And make me Your slave alone.
For it is in perfect submission to You
That I find unrestricted freedom.
And it is when your will reigns supreme,
That I truly find my Self.

From Sense Drunk Life, Back to the Sea

I am but a human, frail and dark
Of foibles and errors do I possess,
But one gift appearing above all those earthly treasures
Stands my desire for Thee Alone.

Minor fiefdoms strive to conquer soul,
Petty princes try to grasp the whole
But no reach can circumference that Kingdom
Shining as my Eternal Abode.

Some day the Rightful Ruler of old
Will again stand preeminent above it all
And reclaim rebellious land.
Standing upon truth and peace we will hear its echo.

Like pied piper of old, will my soul call
To out of control scattered mice of sense drunk life
And lead those pesky critters
Back to the sea that is One for us all.

Now I stand upon that crown of glory,
Freedom at last reigns in my soul
Order restored, with mind, sense, and desire
Brought back into the fold of One.

So, to all my brethren do I call:
"Shy from error and cling unto truth
Let go of all that holds in bondage.
To our Infinite Reach let us be away!"

Until

Chant God's holy Nama.
Until all names resonate His glory.
Visit stone temples in pilgrimage
Until you unlock its inner heart.

Then the world, nay this universe,
Becomes your sacred temple.
See purity in lofty giant groves
Until that same purity is awakened in you.
Let your heart melt in holding a babe
Until sweet innocence is resurrected in your soul.
Become merged in ocean's sunset grandeur
Until infinite expanse finds a gateway within.
The wonders and secrets you seek in this word
Are but reflections of your true self.
Go ahead, seek the Beauty of life,
In its reflected images,
But always remember
Until you find it within
Your search is incomplete
For Reality cannot be permanently found
In its reflected images.

PURIFICATION

The paths are many
The goal is one,
No one path stands above another
Except for the individual seeker.

Paths are many,
Disciplines vary,
Yet all have a similarity
In that they lead one inward.

A focused mind
Stops the constant movement
Of a harried self
And restless thoughts.

In stillness
God's thoughts are revealed
That lift and purify
Heart, mind and soul.

Purification makes one receptive
To the Self Supreme
That loosens and expands bonds
And recovers innocence lost.

At last all past reactions are stilled
Diversity plays on the chest of Unity
Vast freedom rings throughout eternity
And God and man merge into One.

Surrender to Grace

So many teachers
So much advice given
So much said about the path
So much confusion ensues.

Deciphering essence from accident
Truth from falsehood
Reality from delusion
Comes only from knowing the Truth directly.

Until that lofty moment
Truth is inferred
Truth is but glimpsed
Truth remains illusive.

What can be said
To decipher essence from accident
To know the Way
To freedom and Light?

To define the crux of the issue
Needs to be set right
To know what needs to be removed
To allow Truth and Light to shine.

For the light shines already
In deepest recesses of soul
But mind is dull, unreceptive
To its brilliant glow.

The crux of the problem
May be rightly said
To be the ignorance
Of Light's Beauty already aglow.

Proud arrogance of 'I'
A self apart from the whole
Keeps light from shining
In a realized manner known.

But can self remove self?
No, it cannot be so,
What is to be done then
To know Truth alone?

Surrender of self
To a higher power must be
Within comes this deep surrender
Of the absolute rule of 'me and mine.'

All ritual and mental notes
All institutions and position
All mental gymnastics and scripture
Retire helplessly before this knowledge.

Only that movement
That makes 'me and mine' die
Only that which is mutually exclusive
To notion of mine can be right.

Intelligence is not,
Position in the world is not,
Ritual does not do it,
Only surrender provides the key.

For surrender admits
That self cannot do the work,
And only by a higher power
May the self be born again.

This surrender needs to be
Of the deepest sort,
A complete letting go
Of the idea of 'I and mine.'

This surrender cannot be
In words only for show alone,
It cannot be institutionalized
But must be in the heart and soul.

All else of philosophy and religion
Is but a prelude
To this ultimate sacrifice of 'I'
Which alone can make the way.

But, be clear on this
Surrender alone is not the key
But only makes the way
For Grace to enter in.

Grace is the sole power
That brings purity into being.
Grace is the intelligence
That perfectly guides all.

The power and intelligence of Grace
Is working now
To inspire darkened minds
To surrender to all.

To surrender means to let go
Of the notion, 'I am the doer'
To surrender means to let go
And know God's will is supreme.

To surrender is to have perfect faith
That all is as it should be,
To surrender is to fall
And know that loving arms will embrace.

Surrender is the key
All else is but preparation
For that all consuming letting go
And giving heart and mind to the Supreme.

The Seed that Yields Fruits

O Sadhaka
Long does the Master wish to share
Share the wealth of Its heart and soul
The super abundant share of Its Spirit.

It longs for you to receive
To receive all It has to give
But a full pitcher cannot receive
Only when it is empty may it be receptive.

O Sadhaka
Open your heart and mind
Rid it of the contents of the world
And like an opening bud become
The glorious warmth of morning Light.

Open yourselves to quiet yearning
Experientially awaiting the glance of inner Light,
Patiently be that expectancy
For it is not given to the over-anxious.

O Sadhaka
The opening is yours
The Day is ripe for harvest
Of seed that yields such glorious fruits.

Look upon the Mountain High

Look upon the mountain high,
Climb straight up, don't be shy.
Feel the earth on your bare feet,
Keep on going, never know defeat.

Nightly streams of water running,
Recognition of its conscious murmuring.
Move on up the mountain high,
Don't stop, don't die.

Burning sun running through your veins,
Fire purifies and causes pains.
Keep on climbing, it's vital now,
Pain and anguish are part of the Tao.

Freedom now in the sky,
Watch out! That's just a lie.
Wake up, don't be carried away,
This is not where you're supposed to stay.
Keep on climbing though it's steep,
You're almost to the peak.
The Perfect Master is now in view,
Look upon him, you know what to do.

The all-pervading sound is now a roar,
Relax, this word is the door.
Colors abound and turn into one,
Blue is all around,
Now look to the Sun.

Here it comes in bright streaks,
Like a sun coming over a peak.
Then it bursts upon you as the one,
The trip is over, you are done.

Becoming one with the Light,
You end your intense plight.
Now if it is to be, you come back to Earth,
Be careful don't lose your mirth.

Loneliness descends as you come down,
Joy will return, you need not frown.
Spread the message far and wide,
You have seen God's side!

David climbs in all weather, he despairs and catches himself—and as he regains his faith, his inner light holds him strong. He is a seeker, a yogi, traversing the unknown to the personality, the unknown to the ego, but the known to the deep spirit within. He is learning to understand how the Divine manifests in the cosmos, and to him personally through experiences.

To give us perspective here is a view from Sri Aurobindo from *Essays on the Gita*, on this magnificent process.

> How does this Being manifest himself in the cosmos? First as the immutable timeless self omnipresent and all-supporting which is in its eternity being and not becoming. Then, held in that being there is an essential power or spiritual principle of self-becoming svabhava, through which by spiritual self-vision it determines and expresses, creates by liberation all that is latent or contained in its own existence. The power or the energy of that self-becoming looses forth into universal action, Karma, all that is thus determined in the spirit. All creation is this action, is this working of the essential nature, is Karma. But it is developed here in the mutable Nature of intelligence, mind, life, sense and form-objectivity of material phenomenon actually cut off from the absolute light and limited by Ignorance. All its workings become there a sacrifice of the soul in Nature to the supreme Soul secret within her, and the supreme Godhead dwells therefore in all as the master

of their sacrifice, whose presence and power governs it and whose self-knowledge and delight of being receive it. To know this is to have the right knowledge of the universe and the vision of God in the cosmos and to find out the door of escape from the Ignorance. For this knowledge ... enables {a} return to spiritual existence and through it to the supracosmic Reality eternal and luminous above this mutable Nature.
(pg 294–295)

As David, over time, and in degrees, gains this highly intuitive knowledge-understanding he develops a healthy individuated ego, one that can refine and purify and gain confidence in a new expanded, widened and deepened conscious awareness—an ability to witness from a multidimensional perspective, an ability to be personal and impersonal. He is more capable of identifying his fractured or weakened egoic nature, his habitual stances based on personality and the programmed collective consciousness that unthinkingly rules much of our lives. He wakes up. David awakens his self-vision and starts to guide the self-becoming process by knowing when and how to intervene when limited ignorance entices. He is forming an increasingly conscious inner witness that is more and more connected to the light. He takes on increasingly perilous and yet blissful terrain as he climbs

Yogacharya David, Cloud Mountain, Washington, USA. 2001.

Yogacharya David, at Painted Canyon and the Ladders, California, USA. 2017.

Chapter Three
The Path of Conscious Witnessing

The steep and perilous mountain climb brings David glimpses of new wisdom, often after a focused purification. It is as if each step or each new plateau holds for a while and then a new valley arises and he dips into the old world of programmed perception, personality and a less evolved egoic desire nature. Nevertheless, as we study his poems, we see David reformulating a healthy ego, one that can consciously witness inwardly and outwardly. He clearly gifts us with his new-found self-awareness, and his ability to step back and observe, open his heart while tempering his left-brain commands and demands. He is more and more remembering who he really is. As the spinal energy increases, he enters a high-frequency state of Infinite Awareness and can hold this state for longer periods of time.

And, as David shares, this requires a new kind of surrender. Here is what he says in *My Spiritual India*:

> The term 'surrender,' when used for spiritual reasons, is not distinguished between other definitions of the same word in the English language. This can lead to misperceptions of this powerful noble action. In a human sense 'surrender' means to give up. In a spiritual sense when surrendering to God, we may feel weak and unable to continue, but we do not surrender to an enemy who then dominates us out of egoism. Rather, we surrender to an inner force, a Higher Power. In surrendering to that force, we are open to more life, intelligence and vast resources beyond our own power. We are a conscious witness to a flood of newly martialed power that propels and guides us. Not feeling disconnected and lonely as with a human surrender, a spiritual surrender puts us in contact with sublime spiritual realms. We are no longer separate

and alone—we feel a part of all that is. In that unity, forces come to our aid, we feel fulfilled, rising above our circumstances. *(pg. 26—261)*

David continues:

Why be foolish and go it alone when all heaven and earth are at the disposal of the omnipotent One? Why make decisions with only the paltry human reasoning, when the all-consciousness of the omniscient One is ready at hand? Not out of weakness does this surrender come, but out of the profoundest wisdom . . . It is the courage of a true and faithful spiritual warrior that allows for faith in that which is above and beyond self. It is the courage of such a one that leads to freedom through surrender. *(pg. 261)*

Truly the warrior status is developing within David as he speaks of this new consciousness coming forth. Inverting the old idea of surrender, he now understands it as a surrender to a brilliant intelligence, a profound wisdom, a sacred freedom that reaches to the heights of illumination and the heart-depths where the brilliant light of pure soul resides.

I Am the Witness

The alternating world
Passes through my middle
Agony to Ecstasy
And back again.

I feel my oneness
With all humanity
Yet I stand alone
Under uncomprehending gaze.

The world cracks and crumbles
Titanic cataclysmic mass
Tortured twisted forms
Cry out and then are gone.

Unconscious nature and Man
Are feast for
The destroyer's yawning jaws,
All go tumbling in.

The Cosmic Play
Continues inside of me
I witness these forces vast
And I shake with their power.

As witness I feel the screams
Of destructive sounds
And sirens of pain
Reverberating throughout my cells.

I AM the Witness
Of this stupendous play
It all happens inside
Of me.

I cannot move
One microscope inch
From where I see
All this happening.

I cannot flinch
In shock and horror
Or identify
With any passing scene.

My insides twist and tremble
Earthquakes clash and groan
A thousand voices cry out
And then are gone.

Day after day
Apocalypse continues its course
The Destroyer sweeps all away
Leaving only the Witness.

In sudden stillness
All comes to a stop
Peace is known
The shadow loses power and drops.

Then grinding motion
Begins again
The Destroyer
Is grinding His teeth once more.

And so it goes
Without respite
The Witness
Smiles.

O Infinite Presence

O Infinite Presence
So lost do souls become
From Your comforting solace
Lost in woods of confusion.

How is it
That You are so close
So near to heart and breath
With the openness of a child,
That those who are bewildered
Fallen so low
Confused within confusion
Feel forlorn and far from You?

When one knows You
You are the nearest of Friends
The innermost thought
The Life of all Life.

In the Beginning

In the beginning my quest was an
Inarticulate urge toward going beyond
The pain I found myself in.
As time proceeded in my quest
I found the goal became clear.
Now my sweet soul is filled with the
Unlimited Goal of my search.

Pain has turned to joy!
Blindness dropped its blinders and revealed
A Divine Vision!
Graves of yesterday's disorders opened
And dark ghosts have risen into
Angels of Lights.

Lost at Night

When a man is lost at night
There seems no safe place to be found.
Fear and suspicion plague that wanderer.
But when the sun rises all that seemed
Menacing and confusing shortly before
Now are commonplace with understandability.

In the beginning I yearned to understand
But did not have the means.
Now the means and the undying desire
Merge into a state of realization.
What Bliss!

O Infinite Self

O Infinite Self
You manifest as so many masks
They cannot obscure Your Light at all!
Your Light illumines the mask itself
And Lights the way for all to follow.
Jai Purusha!

A Golden Alchemy

The crucible holds all the ingredients,
Containers abound on the earth,
But most are inert to their purpose
Asleep to reality.

A few, here and there
Have a stirring within,
Spirit, the secret ingredient
Begins an involuntary alchemy.

For many it is a spark
A sudden spasm that soon subsides,
A powerful memory it becomes
Fading and overcome by a clamoring world.

A chosen few are started on a journey
A long and difficult sojourn
Of many steps
Without any distance.

Tempting obstacles abound
That would cool the ardor
Of an unreconciled inner action
A path begun but incomplete.

Many resting places, diversion and misbegotten paths
Lie before the awakener,
False peaks, sirens and dragons
Would dissuade and kill the spark.

Very few indeed recover their steps,
Most are caught, ensnared in a web
Of illusions that show lustre
And then dissolve into dust.

Of those that hear the call
Whose spark refuses to die,
Those intrepid warriors for Truth
Will never give up.

A spark becomes a flame,
Flame spreads as a conflagration,
The whole world aflame
Beyond human control.

Searing pain, uplifting Bliss
Merge into a singular flame
A crucible of fire
With a golden core.

Slowly, almost imperceptibly
The gold begins to form,
A gold that cannot be touched,
Only witnessed.

That most treasured bounty
Whose precious few ounces
Can save the entire world
Is at last shining on the earth.

Seducer of Souls

The Course is set before,
It is present in the moments of the day
Demanding the power of our life
The Course is set, it remains always.

The descent requires no effort
Only a decision
It feels free, down hill
Pure fun in its seduction.

Then comes its opposite
Always its opposite,
Looming struggle upwards
After the grand descent.

Peaking the opposition
Comes the next free ride down
Great speed, without thought of consequences
Freedom of the moment.

Then come boomerang shocks
Sadden, then dismay its caught victims.
Bringing darkness of valley's deep
Gum-like glue clings to each step.

"Tis not what I sought!"
Thinks darkness' victim
"Tis not what I expected!"
Echoes the unwise mind.

Then sudden seduction comes
The downhill race,
Each repetition a greater descent
More sticky glue and darker darkness.

O seducer of souls!
You claim victims numberless
Sideways, their glances make normal
Their consequences
Unintentional victims in mass delusion.

Wisdom gained at such cost
Through ad infinitum ups and downs
O costly realization
At lasts reveals the folly.

"The down does not come without a trial
The free ride, alas, not free,"
Looking sideways does no good
Downs always makes for ups.

Oh Wisdom, dare you come to me
Right memory, after untold progression
To regression,
Seek no more finality in the everchanging
Rest no more on the wheel ever turning.

Let Go, Let It Be

Mindful Mind
Senseless Senses
Bodiless Body
Formless Form.

Paradox without reflection
Knowledge without a knower
Wisdom without a witness
Colorless, is that truth?

Mind tries to grasp
Apple carts upturned
Patterns out of synch
Focus without a lens.

Who can know?
Who is left to know?
What knowledge
Where there is no resemblance?

Let go
And let it be
Exist in the moment
Be at once free.

Stillness in silence
Restlessness abate
Cowards at rest
Heroes resurrect.
Om

Four Lions and The Diamond Light

Going to the inward Mind
Four lions lie in wait
Fear, lust, greed and wrath
Waiting, waiting, waiting, the wait!

For a moment, a weakness perceived
Then upon their hapless victims
They pounce to devour their very life!
The life that will make the lions to live again.

Four lions lie in wait
Looking for a moment in time
When they catch a look, a glimmer,
Of lack of resolve gleaming in the eye!

Or doubt it is, that creates a chance
Perhaps loneliness, it makes them lick their chops!
They lie in wait in darkened dale
Where self-pity makes its prisoner an easy prey.

But wait, the lions scurry for cover!
When like-minded aspirants join in on the stroll.
And oh! how those lions detest and are sickened to death
When melodious words are sung to the most-High.

Ah! Here comes a chance, a lovely trap
When ego or pride makes stilts for legs,
Yes, pride places the head high on wobbly peds
"We will not attack till the moment is right,"
Say those wily lions in wait!

O here comes the aspirant riding high
Round corner too fast, head and chin tilted to the sky
Lions in the wait on either side
For unwieldy stride to bring that one down with a crash!

And when the crash comes, as it certainly must come
The trap of shame is sprung,
The game is theirs, the lions have won!
They suck life's blood, down to its very marrow.

And when the gorging is done, but it is never truly done,
They seek to devour corpse and all!
But deep down inside, close to the heart
Resides a spark they can never touch.

It is a spark, a glowing Light
That is oft' clouded by gray and dark,
Is hidden really, never dimmed
For once uncovered, it shines brilliantly as ever again!

The lions, if they could, and they would if they could
Would take away that little diamond of Light
And devour whole, life, ego and corpse!
But they can't, they can't! As much as they would like.

For that Light, that brilliant shining Light,
Cannot be bartered, sold or stolen away
No, not even tarnished, corrupted or even a dent will it know!
For it is forever, and that cannot be changed.

That is your treasure O aspirant!
Gems of realization and spiritual Light of gold.
It is your inheritance that, no, not even you can give it away.
It is a Gift, and it pleases It greatly to give Its Self to you.

So those lions may be there, they can lie in wait
But you've a secret weapon they cannot devour, no, not even in their dreams.
You've defeated those rascal lions, you've beat them square
You need only claim . . . (shall I say it) your lion's share!

Angels Sing

Angels sit around the throne
Singing their praises to You,
Angels come to earth
Making Your will manifest.

Your Throne of Consciousness
Surrounded by pure vibrant thoughts
Ringing with vibrating song
Bliss resounding through and through.

Sound's vibration of Bliss!
Creates forms, architectural design
The carpenter thus builds His universe
With hammer of thoughts and nails of golden energy.

All creation sings Your song
Uplifting purity echoing endlessly,
All creation sings Your song
As tears of joy flow on and on.

O Master Builder
Your Angelic thoughts inspire those
Who walk in Your righteousness
And Listen to You in stillness.

Purify Your Universe
Through Your humble instruments
Bring peace and good will to all
Let Your angels sing forevermore.

Look for the Light

Varied are the forms in this passing night,
And yet it is true all forms come from one Light.
Great is the pageant that passes before us,
Such entertainment when we see the projectionist.

Lights dancing on a giant screen,
Creation, Preservation and Destruction
Reflect on the Light beam.
What is Earth but a passing show;
How many people each day decide to go.

Lack of understanding is the cause of suffering,
Wisdom teaches us the Art of Being.
Wake up your mind to freedom's call.
Be no longer a serpent who has to crawl.
Search way down deep for the peace inside,
And look up for the light in which to abide.
See the Kingdom that is within
Break away from all delusion.

Good Morning

Good Morning!!

The sun's golden light
Just peeking above horizon's altar
Shooting streaming beams
Through misty bows in green
Such thrilling mystery
In a new born day.
Silent majesty for all to see
By humble Artist anon
With no desire
Other than to create
And please the eye
Of the awakened beholder.
May your day be lovely.

The Flower Glories in the Sun

The flower glories in the sun
It proclaims:
"Is there any greater than I?"
And it listens intently to its echo.

The flower, today is, tomorrow is not.
It cares not for the branch that produced it.
It knows not of the trunk that fed it.
It imagines not the roots that made life possible.

It sees the sun
But wants only praise from it,
Receives the breeze as a kiss
Only to increase the blossoms' variety.

Oh small, insignificant flower,
You cannot appreciate
The thousand other blooms around you
You deny yourself the joy of gratitude!

Love Flows all Through and Through

Love flows from me to you,
Love flows all through and through.
I am in God, God is in me,
Oneness of the whole is all I see.

True hearts meet forever in one,
All saints partake of one sun.
Truth reigns throughout the land,
Shushumna is our magic wand.

O dear people see true Love now,
Riding on the human vessel's prow.
Wisdom is at the steering helm,
God's power a' blowing does overwhelm.

Infinite Is Infinite

The Infinite finds expression in the finite,
Water in the ocean is cast liquid
Then sun turns it to gas invisible
Becoming ethereal cloud vapors.

The Infinite plays as the finite
Coming to the next expression of water,
Clouds condense to rain or snowfall
Descending, descending and descending.

The Infinite is frozen-finite,
The snow and rain may form sculptures
Once hardened as ice and snow on earthly plane,
Until quickening transmutes to liquid again.

The Infinite builds movement as the finite,
Snow and rain descend to Mother earth
Gradually gathers as streams, creeks, and rivers
Moving, moving, moving, into greater movement.

The Infinite finds diversity in the finite
The waters of different places blend and meld,
They complete and rush ever on
Seaward to their unknown destination.

The Infinite finds fulfillment in the finite
After a long, long journey of various forms,
Rivers of liquid rivers meet and dissolve
Into liquid ocean, vast and receptive.

Infinite and finite are not different,
Can the ocean and various forms of its manifestation
Be said to be disconnected? Can snowflake be without ocean?
Even though snowflake appears of a different nature?

Breezes Blow

Breezes blow in varied strains
Some carry exciting flavors
Aromas activating, desires coming in rising tides
Never-ending calls of activity.

Other breezes bring complacency
Sleepy indifference to life's duties,
A comatose fog,
Sunk in dark despair.

The world tosses a blinded mind
Upon the alternating waves
Of these two poles
Seemingly endlessly caught.

Enlightened Ones bring hope
Through a sublime alternative
Requiring firm steadfast mind
A heart molded by a higher Light.

Quiet the mind,
An overheated mind finds rest
In a steady breath,
New reflections flash on the
Mirrored lake of awareness
Revealing a truer Light than
The lesser lights of old.

Calm clarity reveals sacred links
To divine origins of the past hidden
Now revealed in lightning glimpses
Thrilling—inspiring—uplifting.

Now the mind purified
Knows the Truth revealed,
The eternal Self is realized
Impurities of ego-self dissolved.

Re-union is now completed
No darkness of separation exists.
The enlightened Self reigns
The eternal extending forever
Finding completeness in its perfect beginnings.

Sacred Language of the Gods

Sacred language of the gods
Intoned in precise measure
Dances ecstatically in the cells
Awakening inner sight.
Sacred language of the gods
Reveals Atman's purity
Destroys ignorance forevermore.

Smile that Everlasting Smile

Smile that everlasting smile,
It makes me smile within.
Smile, that never-ending smile,
It changes us to light from dim.
You know, the joy it brings to all,
So bring it in right now.
It's only your joy,
Your ever-expanding joy, that
Makes me smile within.

The Shepherds' Watch

The night stars glowed overhead
It was lambing season,
And the shepherds kept watch all night
So the lambs would be kept safe.

Some shepherds half dozed,
And some watched the night sky progress
As constellations passed from
Horizon to horizon,
Somehow they knew, sages knew the portends
Of these progressions.

That night they were in awe
For a bright Light was above,
Unbeknownst to them
Three planets combined to
Make a great display.

Distant wise men knew something of this,
The shepherds did not have the training
But they often watched night's rotation
They knew it was special
Knew it meant something.

Those shepherds who kept awake
Were of saintly character,
They went to the temple, kept the commandments
But, perhaps more than that, they kept watch.

For what did they keep watch?
They did not know.
A mystery? Something larger than themselves?
They felt it for a long time now, many years.
A wonderful potential was about to be released.

These simple men
Dressed in rough woolens
Smelled of sheep and nature's soil
Uneducated to the world, but wise in simplicity.

They watched the brightness overhead
And wondered,
Felt a quickening that did not allow sleep,
And they watched
Filled with an expectation unknown.

Then it happened
An opening between this world and another
Like an aurora borealis,
Light danced in the darkened night.

And they felt something,
A thrill and pulsation of energy in the air
That moved with waves of Light
A bit overwhelming—like standing
On the edge of a great height.

Yet that Light seemed to communicate something
A calming that said—"Do not be afraid."
Fascinated they kept watch,
Fully caught up with attention bright.

Then they heard it.
Was it a sound in the air or inside them?
They could not tell
But they heard it and were thrilled.

It was music and voices that sounded
Beautiful—so beautiful—
And indescribable—like nothing they had heard before.
A song without words or melody—and so sweet.

In hearing it some seemed to swoon,
Those hearty shepherds melted in the hearing.
Was it sound or vibration?
Was it a song or bliss?
It was both.

An event of extraordinary dimensions
Was occurring—they had somehow
Known all their lives
That this was going to happen
In fact, it was for this moment they were born.

They knew this now
They knew this was a fulfillment of a promise
That was made from the foundations of the world
This night was meant to be.

Now they were grouped together
The shepherds were themselves herded
By some unknown force,
A majestic power moved them down the hill
They were willing slaves to what was happening now.

This force guided their steps
As they wordlessly moved
They knew the moving Light in the sky
The magnificent strains of music
And this guiding Force were all connected.

Where were they going?
They did not care.
Would they return?
They did not know.
Heaven had opened its flood-gates this night
And they had no will of their own.

Step by step they were herded down the hill
And on that hillside there were caves

Partly dug into the hill
Partly built up with stone and timber.

To one of those caves they came
And somehow the intensity of the feeling of that night
Seemed to be concentrated in that cave
That whatever was going on overhead
Was concerning the inside—right here.

The Light of the 'star'
The rolling Light
The incredible music and this shepherding Force
Was all concentrated here
And they shuddered
For it was powerful—beyond them in too many ways.

They found courage somewhere
And entered in
For all they knew—they would be swallowed
In a great flame of a yawning infinite chasm.

However—that is not what they saw,
Inside this cave a lamp glowed
A smell of damp earth awoke
Them from their shaking,
And some stabled animals made
For a familiar scene.

And there was a family
A man whom they recognized as a tradesman
Probably a carpenter judging by his clothes and hands,
A pretty young wife.

And most amazing—without being amazing
Was their new-born baby boy,
Who drew all of their attention
Once they took in the scene.

At one and the same time
He was an ordinary new-born
Tiny—with tiny sounds
But extraordinary at the same time.

For they knew
This child had drawn them to this place.
The Light in the heavens—
The music—the star—were all heralds for him
And yet—here he lay like a helpless babe.

Their minds reeled back and forth
Heaven and earth
As above, so below
Human and Divine.

Then the babe opened his eyes
And such peace flooded them
A peace that seemed to extend
To all—the whole world.

And their inner quaking stopped
They knew all was well
That they—and all in the word is now blessed
Divinity was born in this tiny form.

And some of them openly wept,
Some prayed out loud,
Some went inside themselves
And new worlds were revealed.

Who was this child?
No history or name
No pedigree did they know
No grand palace in which this princely child was born.

But in simplicity
Seeking shelter in a rough barn
Earthly as they themselves were
Yet connected with the vast events above as well.

The mother and father smiled
In acknowledgement to these shepherds,
As if they understood why they had come in
As if they too were in awe of
These events—of this child
And they nodded to each other as mutual acquaintances.

And now it was time for them to go,
As they slowly backed out
It was like tearing off their own skin to leave,
Yet they knew it was time.

They emerged—as it were—
From the womb of the cave.
But they did not go empty-handed,
For they were changed,
A deep and abiding peace
Lingered around them—never to leave.

They wended their way up the hill wordlessly.
In fact, since they had first observed the star above,
They had been in wordless wonder,
Yet they had moved together as one being.

And now they went to their separate flocks
Without speaking
Filled with awe—
And a joy, and a contentment.

Each one knew they could die—right then,
And die fulfilled.
Many went on to live for more years
Keeping the sacred night
Carefully secure in their hearts.

Who could they tell?
Who would believe them?
What words could describe it?
Sometimes they talked quietly
Among themselves—and they knew.

They knew the truth of what they experienced,
They knew they had acted as one person,
And they had been witness to an event far beyond
Their understanding,
Yet they knew intimately exactly what they had experienced.

They were the shepherds,
Chosen by some inexplicable means
To be witness to events beyond their understanding
Yet they knew it was for that
Process they were born.

The Light Bearer

Guru is the Light
That leads me out of darkness,
Bringing me into the self-same Light
And ever-lasting Freedom.

I have wandered in a dark house
Feeling my way blindly
Not knowing there was anything else
Till one night a light flashed on, then off.

From that moment I knew
There was a secret source
From which Light I could illumine,
Relieving the heavy burden of the night.

O, to find that Source!
A few alluded to it
Fewer still had their eyes opened to it
Yet I remained in blind pain.

After what seemed an eternity of time
I entered a room filled with Light
Or did she enter my room?
I cannot say.

The Light brought hope-bliss!
Yet it also was painful
As my being adjusted to this new light;
A moth flying headlong into the Flame.

O maddening search
As my tiny flame sputtered
When away from that Lighted room,
The light was to me as precious as breath!

When near to her my Light shone brighter,
Further away it sputtered
But it would not go out!
Fueled by an inner pain without remorse.

Finally, finally, finally
It burns more steady
Dampening-fear dries,
Gusting winds of desires die back.

Flame, oh Flame!
The Light Bearer has done her duty
Bringing Light to the darkened,
Igniting ready wicks in souls.

Now O Sadhakas
We must strive and strive
To keep the flame alive
Making the Flame burn steady, bright!

In my inner vision
I see many, many lights
Spreading, glowing, shining!
Spreading, glowing shining!
Illumination enough to make this world
Glow with the Light she had become.

O Infinite Joy

What is this Joy
That comes as a constant refrain
Bubbling as an underground spring
Then rising as a colorful fountain.

What is this Joy
Beyond comparison
To any earthly enjoyment
Self enjoying Self, it must be so.

O what is this Joy
My constant companion
Through day and night it sings
Its divine melody of bliss.

Thoughts are dry in comparison
Worldly relations but a vague reflection,
Words are empty
Unless they spring from that Joy.

This Joy comes from nowhere
It goes to nowhere
It is self-contained
Yet connected to everything.

This Joy needs nothing
Yet it loves to create
Not for any outcome
Except as a fulfillment of itself.

O Incomparable Joy!
I would not trade the world for you
In you I feel complete
And you permeate all that is.

O Incomparable Joy!
Your song in me makes love complete
Makes life sweet
Moves me to my innermost depth.

O Radiant Joy!
I die in you
Losing myself in your glorious song
Becoming an instrument of your movement.

O Joyful Joy!
Ever sing your song of Joy
In your ardent devotees
Merging lover and beloved.

O Infinite Joy!
Like a wave on the ocean
I dance in droplets in gleaming rays
Then plunge and merge into my Mother of Joy.

O Boundless Joy!
I know you alone
I mingle in your might
And dance in ecstatic bliss.

O Endless Joy!
I ever play
Between reflecting your Joy back to You
Then dissolving in unqualified union
Of Your infinite Joy.

Two Paths in the Wilderness

Who are those who shout so loud,
Claiming their exclusive right
For knowing the Infinite One
Saying, "My way is true, all others, false?"

Two paths in the wilderness
One used by deer, another by rabbits
What is suitable for rabbit
Does not permit a deer progress.

Two mountains stand majestic
One is King of mountains,
The other is Queen
Each have his or her legitimate role.

So many examples may be given,
The Form and function of a thing
Must allow for differences
Must vary according to need.

Then why not our approaches to God?
Are there not many Ways?
Does the Divine really listen to the
Name used, ignoring the heart?
Let each tend to his or her own path,
While honoring the way of others.

Dance Divine

Over and Over goes the Dance Divine,
We call for God, we call for God.
The King of Hearts springs to our aid,
And softly chants his healing Amen.

We feel uplifted in his veritable presence,
And off we go to spend his glory on the sense.
In our grossness the Lord retreats,
Content to visit us on another day.

On and on and on we go,
Content to play on the passing show.
But one day the Lord's presence we'll truly miss,
And he'll be dancing for a true heart.

We will cry and weep and gnash our teeth,
But the Lord will say, "He ignored me so,
I will wait for a while this time."
In this time the heart is purified.

The Lord comes at last to the broken heart,
The King of Hearts has delayed no more.
Will you dance with the Lord Divine?
Let us all return home through the Dance Divine.

O God of My Heart

O God of my heart,
Sower of love in every part.
Knower of all things,
All worlds are your makings.

Create in us your perfection,
Let us show you true affection.
For when we are born in Spirit,
Our Love lamps will be truly lit.

Many is the time you show us your Love,
And you lightly descend on us like a dove.
But many prefer things of the world,
And ignore you, the greatest pearl.

But for those who persevere,
Will You make very dear,
And in the dawn when all is clear,
None will have anything to fear.
Intolerance is ignorance matured,
Faith is hope solidified,
Sex is a poor substitute,
For spirituality.

Great Builder of Images in the Mind

Great builder of images in the mind,
Transcending all space and time.
What images create ye?
Thoughts of prison, or do they free?

Creating tomorrows today,
Energy sent to the ether stays.
What molds cast you?
Are they false or are they true?

Incantations of Good and Love?
Curses cast with filth and crud?
What say you O mighty Prince?
Do you build a pretense or Light?

Your subjects run to and fro,
You give up and go with the flow.
No great kingdom here,
All quaking in turmoil and fear.

Break away from anarchy's lie
Rise up, that evil one must die.
Even Death to the Noble Warrior must come,
In order to fully realize the One.

Great builder of images of the mind,
Transcending all space and time.
What images create ye?
Thoughts of prison, or do they free?

Silence is Golden

To be silent, a blessing,
To be still, is to know God,
To know God is to enter Infinite Silence
And come to the peace that surpasses all understanding.

O what a blessing that Silence
But who knows such silence?
Rare is that one
Rarer still the one who lives in that silence.

That silence that resides in your breast
Opening the heart,
Flowing in Peace,
O rare is the one who lives in that peace.

That silence rings in your ears the Amen as Om,
It rings out through time and space,
And as wave upon wave
Silence vibrantly expands in its stillness.

You are that silence, that stillness
From that void has come all that is,
O to be silent, a blessing
To be still is to know God.

We the Children of the Infinite

O Ram, Thou art the Infinite,
All pervading Presence,
How can I hold even a drop of world-knowledge
When my cup already overflows with Your Presence?

You, who wears the stars for Its crown
The milky way is but a path of a few steps
The burst of all creation but a twinkle in your eye
What cup could contain You?

When a man thirsts
He goes to the river with sweet running water
He drinks a little and is satisfied,
He does not need the whole river
Nor does he care for how long the river is.

His need is to quench his thirst
And would he say, "The river belongs only to me,
Only I may drink of it?"
Surely, we would call that man a wretch, a scoundrel.

And what of other rivers with sweet tasting water?
Would we say, "Only my river is worthy,
Your river is polluted, and those who drink it
Will die, will not be given life?"

Surely they drink of their water
And they find it sweet and satisfying,
Is not the value of the river known by this?
We would say of those who say, "Only my river is good,"
To be provincial?

Why do we argue over names?
Are not all names of God equally sweet?
Do not all who drink of these names
Derive its qualities and find satisfaction?

Let us not argue names
But sing of the virtues of the Living Water
And rejoice when another does the same
A brotherhood of the one Living God.

How can ants measure the sun
Other than to say, "It gives our warmth and Light?"
How foolish for the black ants to say to the reds,
"Our sun is true, yours is false."

We need not know how many stars are in the crown
To be in awe at its splendor
And the cup that measures the ocean
Will say, "The ocean is the size of a cup."

We, the children of the Infinite
May rest in the Peace of the Stillness
And melt our boundaries to flood out into unfathomable sea
Until these is not cup, only sea.

Come my brothers and sisters
Be not small minded,
See the vast carpet of starry crown
And be in awe of the majesty that created all.

O Friend of Friends

O Infinite Divine
Beloved Friend of friends
Source of life, wisdom and joy
All creation is in search of You.

Yet where are You to be found?
You grant a glimpse of Yourself here
Then You withhold Yourself there
You tease with a promise, but withhold withall.

You enjoy Your Game,
Anticipation burns in Your devotee
Yet You hide behind a veil
And smile at your own jest.

Is it cruelty or love that motivate You?
Oh! It cannot be cruelty, so it must be love
A love born of anticipation
Knowing the joy of finding will be multiplied many times.

You play Your game
But do You never tire?
When at last Your devotee, in sad repose
Surrenders all, then You come as mother to child.

You embrace, caress and sing sweet songs,
Then You are gone again
With echoes of laughter following
You play your Game.

I tire of the game
I want to find, not seek
I want union, not anticipation
I want You.

O Infinite Splendour
Open my eye to see You shining everywhere
I don't want to behold You in one form
But in all forms.

I want to swim in Your Ocean
Of Sat-Chit-Ananda
And explore the vast Being You Are
Not in separation, but in Oneness of All.

You are with me now
Answer my wish
And let Your Grace
End this separation in Bliss.

O INFINITE COMPASSION

O infinite compassionate
One,
You see to it that Babu,
Your child
Is brought through this
Dark night
You see to it that this
Child of yours
Is Lifted into your joy
And bliss,
That he realizes that
He is not the doer
And that he is forever
In Your loving hands.
Om Sri Ram Jai Ram Jai Jai Ram

Truth Comes in Hidden Ways

Two thieves steal from my inward sight,
Closing my eyes to earthly pleasures and woes
I focus attention on the One
I move inward the spinal Way.

Breathing slows
Mind stills
Heart rests
Hush, calm is here.

Lightning flashes in darkness,
Streams of Om flood silence,
Constrained mind expands,
Blissful joy rises within.

Now inner revelation unfolds,
Unspeakingly Truth makes itself known,
Transformation makes me new
At last I know my Self true.

Truth comes in such hidden Ways,
The world continues its pre-occupations
One here and there hears the call
The world thus-wise becomes enlightened!

Fear to Peace

Fear has fled
Darkness vanished
Desire transcended
Separation healing.

Now:
Peace expansive
Light illuminative
Stillness in the flow
Oneness Everywhere.

A New Day

The chirps of birds herald a new day
Streaks of dawn pierces the dark
Heaviness of night yields
Blessed day begins!

Inner awakenings stir deep
Signs of change come gradual
Yearning outdistances knowing,
Dawn comes too slowly!

I stumble in pre-dawn hours
But see my faults more clearly,
Hope alternates despair
Far too gradually does the sun come!

Sight now awakens
Stronger my steps grow,
I help one here and there
Those whose eyes are darkened still.

A new day dawns
The world awakens
And shakes off the dreamer's trance
Songs of praise resonate from high towers.

The sun is for all
Fear abandons itself to gratitude.
Loneliness becomes omnipresence,
And life knows joy anew!

Hear My Prayer

O majestic Creator of all that is
Hear my prayer to Thee
A prayer that is a heart-burst from my deepest self
Let it rise to Thy exalted, all-powerful,
Compassionate ears and heart.

My deepest prayer to You
Is to absorb my Little self
Into Your great Self
Swallowing me into Your Being.

Reach into me
And take my attachment to things
Making my only attachment to You
Finding rest in only Thee.

Draw up my lust
Take it up high
Into Thy Light
Consummating our union.

You are my beginning and end
Above and below
In front and behind
My all in all and all.

Do not ignore my most earnest of prayers
Respond to me now!
And take this Little one
Making me ever at-one with Thee.

The World Stood on its Head

O Lord I have wealth.
It brought me misery with fleeting happiness.
I have had possessions, the best the world has to offer,
Each was a burden on my back.
I had world authority, even unto life and death,
Each decision ladened me with terrible responsibility.
I waged war and gained immense power
And it became an achor to my soul.

And now, I have no material wealth
And possess immeasurable happiness.
I own little and would happily relieve myself of that.
I feel the lightness of Being,
I have no authority in the world
But there are those who would lay down their lives for mine.
I now wage war on ignorance and wish all to have peace
And my soul is free.

Spirit has turned the world on its head,
Those things I thought would bring pleasure, brought pain instead.
Power that brought fame
Resulted in disturbance and disaster,
Use of force made me a prisoner.
O Lord, free me of worldly gain,
Make me poor in spirit
So I may be rich in You.

Devotees Come

Devotees come for realization
Excited for what is to come
The inner worlds open with a touch
All possibilities lay at their feet.

The honeymoon glow remains
Then fades as the initial lustre
Loses its ease
The path descends into a new season.

The inner world grows darker, colder,
Meanwhile the outer world regains
Some of its lost allure
Tempting to the look and touch.

Forgetting past resolves
Making no claims to previous dreams
The test of resolution stiffens
It is the winter of lost hope.

Many drop away
Littering the path with cast-off disciplines
Bodies tread first right and left
Then back to where they had come.

A few hardy souls tread on
Inner determination drives them
Beyond the borders of sense and reason
An inborn drive that will not die.

Some become stuck in muddy complacence
Too driven to give up
Yet not driven enough to proceed
A kind of spiritual "no man's land."

Others take on painful step after another
Little knowing of what is progress
Only knowing they must go on
From day to day, year to year.

One day the sun rises fair
A spring day's breeze inspires
Blossoms texture the ground
And hope resurrects a new lease.

How many seasons are there to endure?
Dark winters followed by bright spring?
None can tell the wearied traveler
Only that one must go on!

David commits to the climb over and over, commits to never bowing to the shadow-destroyer who grinds away at the spiritual truth, freedom and light. David speaks of how many are caught, "ensnared in a web of illusions that show lustre and then dissolve into dust." He seeks for and becomes an "intrepid warrior of Truth" who refuses to give up. Yes, with "searing pain" alternating with "uplifting Bliss" he undergoes a "crucible of fire" as he witnesses a golden core forming. Even amongst the unrelenting Destroyer at work grinding, David still can "smile" and become ready for the Homecoming.

Yogacharya David, Anandashram, S. India. 2002.

Yogacharya David in St. Thomas Cave, S. India. 2005.

Chapter Four
Homecoming

As we reach Homecoming in our journey with David, we have journeyed far—and in reverence it is easy to acknowledge that this is one mountain! One rare sacred mountain. No wonder so few tackle heights. No wonder so many get caught in the mesh of the finite, the material, and the daily joys and travails. For this also is part of living, and in reverence to the living earth, we also owe her benediction for caring for us as we ought to care for her. Yet, there are the vaster reaches of spirit awaiting our awakening so we can be truly universal in our view and in our every thought and behavior. As Mother Hamilton affirmed: "I am both human and Divine." So with David, and his very explicit hope for us all. Crucial to this journey is the finding of Truth in its many dimensions. David speaks to his notion of truth on this sacred journey.

Truth enters through the door of the mind. Some invite Truth into their hearts, a very few know it in their bones. For the greatest, Truth becomes the fabric of their own Being, until their Being sings the song of Truth to the universe, and the universe in turn sings Truth back to the Soul; the Soul and the universe made one by their song of Truth.

When living in the world we acknowledge dualism to the degree that we are in service to our beloveds. However, the underlying knowledge and Spirit is the unifying vision of one life, one existence, a feeling of the All and All in All. We may then act as God moves through us. We may take action, even strong action toward another, and inwardly know that it is but God meeting God.

Then, why act? Because when we are clear, the creative Spirit can move through us, supporting both our individuation as a unique being while helping us to do our part—live our Dharma.

Homecomings increase in intensity as the spiritual churning progresses, interweaving the call and the response, purification, and a growing refinement of consciousness in witness mode. Yet, the grinding attacks of the Destroyer have not retreated. Destroyer is there awaiting the weak moment. The blessing is a much stronger conscious Witness who can smile at the dark forces that sneak, slither and hover, awaiting their moment as did the lions in the previous poem. Temptation continues. However, the light recognizes it sooner and swiftly demolishes. As the purification process builds momentum, soon nothing is more fulfilling than the sweet inner music of the Divine.

Sadhaka's Homecoming

O Sadhaka
Have you heard the inner music?
Have you not yet seen the lightning flash?
These, O Sadhaka, are leading you home.

Your home within
Your home in eternity
Your home, your very sweet home
Won't you visit it, not even once?

But be warned!
On that journey of a million and no miles
Storms will wreck you
And shaken will you be.

But take heart!
You are not destroyed
Sun will replace darkness
You will know your home.

And ah, the homecoming!
Stars will twinkle their welcome, moon glows warmly,
And oh sun, like a thousand suns
But does not burn or scorch at all.

And angels will sing thrills of joy
When you are in that home of eternal joy.
The way will seem as nothing once there
And all sorrows are swallowed in halos of Peace.

O Divine Mother Your Spirit is Universal

O Divine Mother
Your spirit is universal
The colossal universe has sprung
From Your Being.
You are creator, sustainer and
Destroyer of all that is,
Absorb me in Your Being
Make me complete in Thee.

O Divine Mother
I have sought you without
But it has ultimately brought only tears
and pain.
Make me seek You within
That I might find the everlasting
Glory of Your Presence
Residing within my whole Being.

O Divine Mother
You are my completeness,
You alone can make me whole,
Absorb this little me into
The Infinite You.

O Divine Mother
Keep me in Your Being
Now and always.
Om Peace Bliss Amen

I Stood Upon a Rock

For Eons prophets have proclaimed it
The hearts and minds of aspirants everywhere
Have been quickened by its intimations
All souls have secretly yearned for it.

From this bold entrance
Of the ancient One
Came illumination, and
Sure affirmation of the
Wisdom of the ages.

The knowledge, "I know and
I know that I know"
Rang like a clear, pure tone.
I stood upon a rock
A rock of ageless beauty
Made of Eternity itself.

Shining Like a Tiny Sun

This body is perfect
Every cell
Shines like a tiny sun
Blazing forth
Life, energy and health
In God
This body is perfect!

Thou Art Ever With Me

In sickness and in health,
In prosperity or in need,
In high states or low,
Lord, Thou art ever with me.

Words cannot define You
And philosophies cannot contain You,
Movements cannot exclusively claim You
Lord, Thou art ever with me.

As a mirror catches glints of the sun
A gem may radiate light's beauty anew,
And a lump of coal may become fire itself,
So, Oh Lord, Thou art ever with me.

Now Beauty settles into my Soul
Your embers glow through every occasion
A knowing beyond mind reveals Itself
In these ways, and so many more,
I know, Thou art ever with me.

In God Is My Abundance

In God
Abundance flows to me
Like a mighty river
All comes through me,
Creative thoughts
Positive feelings
Health and vitality
Fills my cup to overflowing,
Bliss and wisdom know no bounds
In God
Abundance flows to me.

SHINING GRACE

O Infinite Grace,
You have killed this little self
And resurrected my greater Self.
May this Grace continue to shine.
Shine so as to burn seeds of attachment to ashes,
And shine to grow new seeds of spiritual understanding.
Shine in all your Glory.
Shine on all, and make thousands
Know Your Universal Vision.
Om Peace Bliss Amen

CRYSTAL DEVOTION

Pearls of Love adorn my heart,
Crystal Devotion fills every part.
Gold of Spirit surrounds my jewels,
Silver-like wisdom reflects in shining pools.

These are my treasure,
Abounding without measure.
Built without hands or labor,
Taking from none and given without favor.

I spend freely of my gifts,
I give to all regardless of merits.
For I in no way deserve what I have,
Finding the treasure neither for being good or bad.

I have one claim to these riches alone,
Only one reason have I known.
This is my inheritance for which I file,
For you see, I am God's own child.

No Bubble Only Sea

O Lord
Make me seek my oneness in Thee
Knowing in You I become one with all,
My desire for union complete
The river at last meets infinite Sea.

O Lord
Make me know Thou and I eternally joined
Ever existent, without end
Alpha and Omega am I in You
Forever united, Forever and ever one.

O Lord
Surcharge Thy will through mine
Make Thy Power flow in me,
Dynamic Life Force overcomes darkness
Allowing Your perfect will expression in and through me!

O Lord
Love is Your true name
Without limit, All powerful
Healer of misery, salve of the soul
Melting self into ever expanding Yourself
Oh, compassionate love.

O Lord
Make me know and speak the truth
Wisdom ring in thought, word and deed
Vibrant with Your power and beauty
Make my words resonant with Your Wordless Word.

O Infinite Master
Make Thy stream of Consciousness be mine
In all things art we together,
For I have made myself totally surrendered to Thee

Thou and I melded,
Even as master musician playing His beloved instrument.

O Absolute
No bubble, only Sea,
No I only Thou,
No encasement, no form
Only vast freedom, only One.

THE LOVER

The lover first hears about his Beloved,
A whisper—a notion—
So familiar yet seemingly far away,
But conceived in the mind and heart.

The lover travels the hard path,
Now stands outside the city gates
Where his Beloved resides
Yearning intensifies.

The lover is now in the ante-chamber
Trembling with desire.
Yet the Beloved has never been further away,
For the lover is anxiously on the brink.

Finally, finally, finally!
The lover lays his head on the lap of his Beloved.
Ah, blessed assurance is known.
The Beloved sings sweet joy-love to Her lover.

A blissful wave sweeps the lover
Into the ocean of the Beloved.
Lover and Beloved merge,
Commingle as One, yet remain as two.

Even as a great river
Retains itself far out into the ocean,
So does the lover maintain an 'I',
Till river completely is lovingly absorbed.

Now, dear lover, the destiny of the drop
Raining from the sky
Is to return to its mother, the sea.
Yet, the journey is full of suspense.

There can be no doubt, however,
The ultimate fate of the drop
Is promised for re-union.
So too, for you O valiant one.
So too for you.

Upward Beauty

Upward Beauty
Send forth your bliss
Make yourself known.

Upward Beauty
Light revealed
Unto me, greatness shown.

Upward Beauty
Thunderous roar,
Infinite seeds sown.

Upward Beauty
Revealing at once,
Your eternal splendors known.

My Purnima Moon

O, sacred Guru Purnima,
You are the lofty moon-Spirit full.
You are high in the heavens
Drawing all attuned souls to you.

Symbol of enlightenment,
Stealer of devotee's hearts,
Your Light illumines the night
And makes all safe in your brilliant orb.

O, Guru Purnima, I bow to you.
You are the sages of all the ages,
Standing shoulder upon shoulder
In ever heightening glory.

Your Infinite wisdom comes to me as
My very own dearest Guru
Secured in the center of my heart.
No longer veiled, you are with me
Always and forever in the center of my soul.
(Even now.)

I write to you as a child,
Whatever my heart says,
For I can do nothing else.
I am your das, your freely given slave,
And through my slavery
You have freed me into eternity.

Hail to Thee

My divine Friend is rounding the corner.
Even from a distance He is bright as the sun!
Hail to Thee, my good Fellow.
Hail to Thee, it is a springtime meeting.

You draw closer, I fall in a swoon.
You come to me in sweetness of love.
Oh, can I contain it all?
No, I burst asunder!

In those flying pieces,
I scatter amongst the stars!
There is no end, because there is no beginning
Freedom, freedom at last.
The great 'I' stands revealed.

Suffocating are name and ego identity
Claustrophobic is psychic knowing,
Even an idea is confining
Only in the uncreated is there room enough.

Blessed Spirit thank you for coming to me.
Thank you for drawing Yourself to Yourself.
You are the Alpha and Omega
And much, much more, and in You
I have the greatest re-union.

Lord Reveal Thyself

All life rises to the top
Beautiful pearl Light appears
O Lord, reveal Thyself, reveal Thyself
Alone I await on You.

Absorbed in sweet contemplation
With Still breath
Alone I await on You
O Please come to me my lord.

Your All-powerful inner force
Draws me to ever-illumined planes
Purifying the wells of my Being
O Lord reveal Thyself, reveal Thyself.

Ever onward You call to me
All the Earth stops,
Humble in awe
Alone, I await in You alone.

O Unfathomable Lord

Om Sri Ram Jai Ram Jai Jai Ram
O Lord
You are purna complete.
To surrendered ones
You satisfy all the soul's
Yearning
In Your tender care,
You also thrill the human
In us with solicitude.
How unfathomable You are
Human and Divine merge
In Your Infinite Self.

A Voice Rang Out

A voice rang out from the mighty Deep,
"Tell all of what you see
Tell them that they too
Have Eternity dwelling within
Their Temple."

This the Voice vibrated from the Deep
In all Love and Compassion
Reaching out to those
Whose ears are attuned to
Such knowledge.

The Power now became an ember glow
Illuminating all the realm
Filling all space with Peace and Joy
A Presence that is forever and forevermore.

The Vibrant Name

Name of God
Is sweetness itself,
The Name enters in
And resonates as bliss.

Nothing compares
To the vibration felt
In spine and soul
As the Name vibrates within.

O blessed devotee,
Do you feel it as well?
The joyful freedom
During the day and deepest night!

Come, let us sing together
In silent harmony,
God is the infinite tune
In rhythm with eternity.

At Every Turn—Beauty

At every turn new beauty abounds,
Leaves burned in orange, gold and red,
A bright moon over-stays the sunrise
Clouds look aflame in the sky blue.

Oh God beautiful, at Thy feet, I do bow,
Ecstatic thrills burst from my heart,
In a feeling of oneness my spirit expands
Love fills the beauteous creation.

Oh, paltry words, sound as a tinkling bell
Compared with the vast boom of creations song,
Limitless Spirit is Bliss without end
And Invisible tears are the bleeding of my heart.

Hail to the Infinite

Hail to the Infinite!
Truest friend
Dearest Lover
Of unlimited Nature,
Oh, how can inscriptions portray
The magnificent vision Thou art?
No, no words will tell
The grandness of what You are.

The human vision says but little
Of Your glory that is ever new,
The little mind cannot grasp
Your true nature and Spirit.

However, what defies imagination most of all
Is the power of Your Grace
That lifts awareness past the limited mind
Past the senses, beyond the known world.

Through super-sensory experience
Your power touches my inmost Being
It expands this little 'I'
That melts into Your infinite Self.

No longer defined
By 'I,' 'me' and 'mine'
No longer contained
By ego's bubble-prison.

The bubble dissolves
'I and Thou' merge
Limitless expanse dissolves, horizon lost,
Joy bubbles forth as silent laughter.

Freedom, freedom is in that Joy!
My Spirit permeates everywhere

Compassionate Love saturates existence
Stillness resounds throughout.

My Soul never tires
Of this Joyful union,
A lover's touch you give
Magnified thousands by thousands.

You convey Your wisdom
Through my awareness,
It unfolds on the mind
As the petals reveal the flower.

You sweep me up as upon angel wings
Into a mystic sky,
Then plunge me into the depthless deep
In an ocean of profound peace.

Oh indeed, hail to the Infinite!
I am lost in Thy boundless embrace
I say 'I' but who or what is this 'I'
But an expression of Thy very Self?
You have become me
Now I have become You!
A Yogi consumed in union
A Son of God enthroned in his Father's mansion.

A Mystic Embrace

I made love to the world
In a mystic union embrace,
And I exploded myself in its womb
Emptying myself in the One.

My soul released from human chains
And radiated Light throughout,
The darkened earthy orb
Mingling my cells with her elements.

My body the earth
Rises in budded trees,
It moves in liquid ocean
And rises in the air to touch the sky.

My concerns are those of the earth
I merge in the fabric of her being,
Her pain is my own
Strength radiates from her core.

I am that I Am
A hallowed movement
The deepest of knowing
And the essence of nature.

How can I know this?
Through Grace unleashed,
A love transformed
And a bliss fulfilled.

Awakening

Morning Sun reveals the Light
Dispelling darkness's gloom,
Wondrous warmth envelopes the earth
And awakens all the world.

Clouds illumined, Golden hues do glow
Revealing the glory of what is to come,
Sounds heard at the early morn
Further unmasks death's nightly dark.

Contrasting with sky dark Blue
Showing Infinities reach stretching all bounds
Of dense clod of clay bounded in space
Taking eye and mind to vital essence.

Unveiling yonder eastern morning star
Bright silver shining door,
Manifesting light from that distant fiery orb
Bringing attention to single pointed intensity.

When suddenly bursts upon horizon's altar
Sun's blazing light of lights
Overwhelming, life giving, illuminating!
Bringing comfort and guidance to wayfarers all.

Wanderers of this earthly place
Hear loves awakening call
See how distant light pierces darkening veil
And leads you aright to your perennial Home.

You are Purna

O Lord
You are purna, complete.
To surrendered ones
You satisfy all the soul's yearning
In Your tender care,
You also thrill the human in us with such solicitude
How unfathomable You are,
Human and Divine merge in Your Infinite Self.

Your Light Illumines

O Infinite Self
You manifest as so many masks
Yet some masks
Cannot obscure Your Light at All!
Your Light illumines the
Mask itself
And lights the way for
All to follow.
Jai Purusha

God is the Beautiful

God is the Beautiful
His sacred Presence
Brings a gorgeous Love
Converting every cell into a singing Angel!

O God is the Beautiful
At His wondrous Touch
All past sufferings
Alchemize into golden Bliss.

Within me, within every one of us
Resides the deepest secret
A secret of the Ages
An unspoken secret of Beauty.

Yes, God is the Beautiful
And His Angels of all creation
Sing His devotional vibration
Proclaiming ever more His unending Beauty!

LET YOUR WILL REIGN SUPREME

It is your Will that acts through this form
You bring whom you will
You take whom you will away
Of what concern is that to me?

All forms are Your forms
All happiness according to Thy Will,
I have but to reside in You within
Reside as Witness to what You do.

I cannot concern myself for what may happen
For all happens at Thy instance
Take all that I have called me and mine
And swallow those into Your Self.

A One without a second,
O ecstatic Love You bring to me,
Oneness of boundless Joy
You fill this cup that is Yours with measureless Bliss.

Gone are past sorrows,
Evaporated future fears,
Only You now exist
Forever make me one with Thy own.

And in oneness who writes this,
As if there are two?
It is You, You in this form,
Also plays as if there is a lover and beloved
Lover and beloved are one and interchangeable.

You make me write on, Beloved
Without scope or desire
Other than to express You
To feel You flow through these veins, muscles and thoughts.

This body that You have created
That You sustain
That You make to dance to Your tune
That You raise to enlightenment.

O Blessed of one Spirit
Let us all reside in Oneness;
Let us also play as two in One
And know total Joy in the play of
Many and as the One.

For my Beloved, You are none other,
None other but the One
Who plays the many
But is always the One.

All Glories be to You, Lord

O my beloved Ram,
How I Love and Adore you.
You are the Light of my life,
Love of my heart, you are my all in all.
Thou art all compassion and love,
Glory is all yours,
Your humility is matchless.

To a disbelieving world you give yourself.
Our selfishness and greed tramples
Your grace while we call for you.
Like a mist the ego shrouds our vision,
It clouds our mind and causes misery.
But through your love, your melting love,
The fog evaporates and the ice melts from our hearts.
Then do we see your shining face.
All glories be to you, Lord.

Flowers of My Dreams

The Flowers of my dreams
Are blooming on my altar for thee
For thou hast seen my piteous cries
And bent Yourself to lift me up.

Who can say how sweet Your sweetness is?
Who can tell of Your glorious mantle white?
Who can serve as they ought to serve
The Light of unspeakable Beauty You are?

Fathomless is the love I feel for You my Lord
Breathless my adoration at Your feet
Why? Because touching You I feel Your Nature
Breathing in I taste Your nectar Presence.

And, in touching You, tasting You
My Soul melts into Your Being
And naturally so, for your lover,
I feel myself spreading over Your
Fathomless, breathless nature.

A Nature so vast, no bird could wing,
A Beauty so rapturous, no artist could paint,
A compassionate Empathy, no saint could ever tell,
A love indescribable, no earthly Love could approximate.

I die—I die my Soul into Your Being!
And as I do, You are writing these very
Words with your own hand.
Your love breaks this tiny human heart
Into a million prisms of Light that continue
To sing your Name evermore.

All in One

Enter gently
The inner Temple

With pure intent
Upon the One

Focus attention inwardly
Upon the single eye

Stable is the mind
Drawing one step closer

Moving deeper now
The Whole attention inward

Absorbed, absorbed
In inner space absorbed

The Light draws one further
Guiding the way

The Sound
Calls one to holiness

Becoming absorbed even deeper
Into the inner stillness

Being is vast
Being is small

Being rests
And creates

Being is at rest
And revelations flow

Being is without movement
And creations burst

Being is without compare
And is seen as the reflection that is All

God is Being
And I am That

I am the I Am
Of all selves

And all is part of the whole
And each makes up the whole

The seed becomes the tree
And the tree becomes the seed

And all is One
All is One

The dreamer awakens
And knows all is One

And One is Peace
And One is Joy

One is Self aware
And One Knows that It knows.

I Saw an Angel Today

Lo, I saw an Angel today,
Fair, haloed with lightness and love,
She appeared in my awesome dream,
Dressed in whiteness and peace like a dove.

Distant memories awoke,
Remembrance of deep friendship spoke,
Hail to thee, my dear friend,
After long separation, we meet again.

Like friends meeting for summertime,
We greet one another with laughter
For time spent apart we do not pine,
What does this matter.

I know you well all the way through,
Your Love and mine we always knew,
Would rise up into oneness of heart
And in that end, find God's fullness
No longer ever apart.

What Presence Moves Within

What Presence Moves within?
Little do I know or realize
What wonders will come
In creeping Lightning streaks.

"Behold I stand at the door and knock"
But who opens,
Who will open,
To inner Light and Beauty?

I, I open
Not to go out!
But to let Him in
I receive Him.

And in that communion
Of heart, of soul, of Spirit
A spiritual feast ensues
Filled with love, wisdom, joy!

O what promise is there
To you and to me
But . . . who opens
Who will open?

The feast is spread
And, who will receive
The universal one
Who knocks at our door?

Yearning

A man of sorrows
Is he who yearns
But does not find.

A worldly man yearns
For fortune found
on the earth.

A man of intellect
Yearns for knowledge
To make him understand.

A sensual man yearns
For titillation of the senses
And gratification of desires.

So many yearnings
Captivate the soul
That leads to more yearning.

There is but one yearning
Leading to fulfillment
As the river finding the sea.

That yearning is inexpressible
Yet has given birth
To millions of expressions.

When infinite Grace
Grants such yearning
As a fire that consumes a log.

Then the one who yearns
Willingly yields all
To that loving conflagration.

When all is surrendered
One alters the threshing floor
Sifting purity from dross.

Until at last
What is left
Is consumed.

Spirit partakes of spirit
Yearning finds its own end
And sorrow transmutes to Bliss.

Ah! Earthly children
All proceeds to the consummation,
Eternity stands with open mouth.

Drops of Eternity
Fill the cup
Filled with the mundane.

It drops and flows
All around
Seeking entry through a closed door.

Desire, fear, anger and sorrow
Fill the cup to rim and more
Leaving not a drop of room.

When mind quiets
And receives a drop
It quickly expels it out.

What waste, lamentable waste
Yet Eternity is patient
Ever dropping Itself.

When a cup opens
And keeps itself so
What Joy, for Giver and Receiver.

A drop turns to flow
The cup overflows
The drop becomes the Ocean.
Bliss is ever so!

Upon a Golden Sea of Silence

Upon a Golden Sea of Silence
I ride wave upon wave of Light,
I feel this little self
In this Golden Sea of Light.

I say 'I,' yet
The 'I' is also the Sea
Vast, open, unending,
It is the whole world and beyond.

I focus upon the self, the witness,
And I am that,
Empty of thought, empty of desire,
I focus upon the Sea, and I am that.

The Sea is peace, stillness,
Yet it moves and contains all creation
It is action, it is actionless,
Simultaneously, without contradiction.

Upon a Golden Sea of Silence
I ride upon a wave of Light
And herein does creation find salvation
As self re-knows its origin in Truth.

The self of self re-remembers
And knows who and what it is.

Miracles and Mariners

You ask of miracles?
What can I say of miracles
That cannot be spoken of
In the softness of a rose petal
Or announced in a sunrise?

Miracles abound, yet we think them ordinary,
Miracles abound, yet minds are blunted,
Miracles do abound.
But these, these be miracles
That a seed grows to a mighty tree,
Natural laws work day in and day out
That a babe can be conceived and grow in a womb.

And, if these leave us wanting more
Then surely God's ingenuity,
Ingenuity that created ocean and plain
Form and Formlessness
Will add to what already is vast treasure.

And one, once taken within
There grows mysteries more.
As without, so within
What this world shows
Is but a reflection
Of vast inner worlds.
So, let me enunciate
Some of those miracles within
As you can only know them
From experience without
Unless you too have been mariners
Sailing vast seas of inner oceans:
Oceanic Consciousness, Oceanic Beatitude,
Oceanic in scope, Oceanic in depth.

Let me tell sailors bold
Sailors who have made the journey
And sailors who are planning
But not to those who only talk, and never do.

Stars, stars shine as if from distance
But really near, and approach,
And then to burst into supernova
That sets the sailor riding amongst waves flight.

Wave after expanding wave,
Till lost in splendour
Till lost to self
Yet finding a true home of light and freedom.

What miracle of miracles
Can this star once bring,
And leave body and intellect still
As consciousness soars?

Then comes cosmic sirens' song
The sound of waters rushing,
Or flute playing high tune,
And bumble bee in low drone.

Or celestial symphony in heart breaking thralls,
And high rising bell heard right, then all around,
Blessed music, cadence of spheres,
Awareness sent expanding in widening rings.

Light and sound, yet miraculously
Without wave or particle needed,
And no outer eye or ear perceived
Miracle of miracles.

Yet those of sound reason and worldly nature
Claim illusion, hallucination, deception
For it fails to fit test tube reduction,
And I say, thank you Lord for making it so.

For such food is for soul, not intellect
It is to expand consciousness, not confirm it,
It is to enlighten, not give tidbits of knowledge,
It informs of truths eternal, not momentary blips.

So, I say thank you, thank you for making it so
Thank you for mysteries that challenge us to the core,
Thank you for miracles in the great and bold,
And thank you for miracles in the common and the small.

For all, all is expression
Of Your magic making power,
All are Your manifestation
Of one life, one wisdom, one love.

For the greatest miracle, the greatest of them all
Is that Your perfect Presence is embedded
Within each and every part
Throughout the cosmic whole.

This then, this is your son
Only begotten, eternal and One,
And to add, add to this, miracle of miracles
You have given it to humankind to know this beyond all doubt.

For in the heart, the heart of all
Can we hear the rhythms of that mighty rush of waters,
For there is hearing without ears
And seeing without eyes.

There is feeling without nerves,
And smelling and taste without nose and tongue,
And Love without physical heart,
All these are possible to mariners brave and bold.

Yet, who is there, who is there to go
Beyond the ordinary and challenge the heights,
And seed brave new worlds
As explorers of old?

To find worlds of promise
And golden treasure not sold,
And Fountains of youth and life
And wisdom of the ages.

So come, come all of ye mariners
Come one and all
Let us seek for these wonders
And miracles that give life.

And in doing, giving life and limb
To causes just and worthy,
Letting go of old ways
And finding an inner glory.

Unlike explorers of old we go not to conquer
But we overcome in order to surrender,
And we die so that we may live,
And we let go so that we might embrace all.

So, lift up your minds to inner miracles
Lift them on high,
Set your mariner's course
And set sail on this lonely night.

LIGHT OF THE WORLD

Behold the Light of the world!
The world is permeated by it, but knowest it not.
Peace reaches past discord into the vast reaches of the Soul.
O come with me; feel your profound oneness with the All.
Simply let yourself live in Divine-awareness.
Down, down, down sinks "the peace that surpasseth all understanding."
Come, come with me, O divers of the Deep.
Come and know your unending Glory in the newborn Son.
On this sacred night, once and for all lose yourselves in Sacred Love.
Om Shanti Shanti Shanti

UNIVERSAL VISION

All of this creation and all it contains
Emerged from this Self and moves within It.
Stand before It trembling
As if before a bolt of lightning.
Who knows this to be true,
Gains immortality.

In reverence of That,
Fire burns
And the sunshine shines.
In reverence of That,
Even the mightiest among us move
As the wind moves.
Why, even death continues
In reverence of That.

When you perceive That
While embodied here on earth
Then you become eternally free.
Not perceiving That
You remain in the world of birth and death.

Homecoming as an aspect of the Universal Vision has been described by spiritual masters throughout the ages. Each master has a unique experience of the Universal and each will use his or her own words to describe the un-nameable immanent and universal, immortal, omniscient, and omnipotent All. David has shared his subjective awareness of this illumined consciousness as it enveloped him in innumerable experiences over the years through his poems. The first stanza of Universal Vision affirms his vast view from the mountain top—the highest peak of the sacred mountain.

> All of this creation and all it contains
> Emerged from this Self and moves within It.
> Stand before It trembling
> As if before a bolt of lightning
> Who knows this to be true,
> Gains immortality.

Throughout his experiences, and through the forty-five years of commitment, David was in prayer often, sometimes continuously. Thankfully he wrote some of his prayers for us to work with to kindle our inner fire, the soul-light, for us to utilize to build our Guru-knowledge and sacred dedication to the highest and best for humankind.

Yogacharya David, Cloud Mountain, Washington, USA. 2000.

Yogacharya David, Cloud Mountain, Washington, USA. 2001.

Chapter Five
Prayers

David wrote many poems that are prayers and it could be said that much of his poetry is a prayer at multiple levels. Selected here are poems that support prayerful inner focus. We start with a touching letter from God to David that David wrote in April of 2014.

Letter from God to me
My child, do you realize that I have always loved you—first in the embrace of your mother rocking you to sleep—then in the protection offered by your father that he would take care, protect you, or teach you how to protect yourself? When your grade one teacher took you under her gentle wings and made you feel special. Then I came to you in church so you could feel my presence and know that I was your refuge. I was always there; when your life was at stake, I rescued you. Even when times got hard and clouds were dark, I called you and you heard me, and we spent time together in the Light.

   I want to tell you that I am always there and that you can always rely on me. All you have to do is call me into the picture, surrender your will to my will. I love you and pass that love to others through you. I am joy, laughter echoing in your soul. I have always been with you but you haven't always been home, or have forgotten that I was worthy and that you could beckon me into your life. Now is the time to have me move in once and for all.

   I can take a lot of room in your life or I can hide as this small voice from far away. I am always there however. Listen, look, search for me at all times.

I am all in all—this bird flying towards you is bringing you my love, is a sign of my presence surrounding you. In the mist I hide my body, in the rain I pour my grace, in the forest I rise and take a firm stand, in the lake I flow.

>Fly with me my child
>I will take you to new heights
>Over the forest so green
>Where I take a stand
>And rise to heaven,
>Listen to the tapping of the rain.
>Om Sri Ram Jai Ram
>
>Here I am
>Seek me in the mist,
>I am the mystic praying for you,
>Follow me down to the lake
>I will take you to the Source,
>And when you think that I am no longer with you
>Call me like the loon
>With a haunting and lamenting sound
>Piercing through the night
>And know that I will come
>And be at once One with You
>With all the love
>you may imagine
>Yours forever
>God

We continue now with David's sacred communication with the Divine.

O Lord

O Lord, Thou hast given me intelligence, reason and feeling.
Please, O Lord, guide Thou my intelligence, reason and feeling.
Thou hast also given power of will, movement, creativity and energy.
Please, O Lord, guide me in the use of will, movement, creativity and energy.

O Lord, finally you have given me things material: money, home, family and friends, and all possessions.
O Lord, make me a good steward of things material and a worthy member of the human race.

Thank You, Lord, for hearing my prayer, for I know You know my thoughts even before I do.
But I pray this prayer to impress it into my own mind.
I pray not to change You. I pray to change myself!

Prayer

O, Lord, You have made me to come here. By Your direction I know this is the right place for me. You are my sole guide and comforter. The masters stand about me, and I know I am not alone. You are my strength and shield.

Infinite Merciful One, I know You are the Supreme Self, the One who acts through all, does through all. You see to it that those who sorrow will be comforted. Those who keenly feel loss shall turn to You and know Your Presence. I release them into Your Keeping!

O Blessed One, bless me always with sure knowledge that we are one, and in that knowledge, Oneness with All in All. Be it so!

Make Me One With Thee

O Lord, Infinite Divine Mother,
Raise me to Your ultimate realization—
Universal Vision—
And make me one with Thee.

Cure Me of Ego

O Mother,
Cure me of the ego-centered idea.
Collapse this ego,
Make me Thy child, as I truly am.

Teach Me to See That It Is You

O Divine Mother,
Teach me to see it is You
Who is hiding behind the mask of creation.
In pulling down the mask,
The Mother alone is revealed.
O sweet Purushottama Papa,
Manifest your vision in me.
Make me see God as both manifest and unmanifest,
Without a break or flaw.
Om Sri Ram Jai Ram Jai Jai Ram

O Lord Protect Me

Surround me in Your Light
Make my defense swift and sure
In You I have my peace and freedom.
Om Peace Om Shanti

The Shining Sword Revealed

O Preserver of the Light,
You are removing the veils of ignorance that cover the soul,
Like the removal of layered sheaths covering a brilliantly shining sword.
You are setting me free in Your Spirit.
I have assessed my desires, and there is no desire in me other than for You.
Tempt me as You might, cover me with ignorance,
Your Light will always emerge from every encasement.
Om Sri Ram Jai Ram Jai Jai Ram

Coming Through the Darkness

May all sincere souls,
During their dark night of the soul,
Stay true to their path of Self-realization.
Treading step by step,
Until they come through darkness,
And into the pure light
Of everlasting love and wisdom.
Om Peace Bliss Amen

O Lord Make Yourself Known

I do not like this game of hide and seek
Come now into Thy child's lonely heart,
Make Yourself known
And the sun shine upon this one,
Be no miser of Spirit
But gracious evermore
O Lord I do not like this game
Come to me now!

Prayer to Divine Mother

O Divine Mother
Purify my love for Thee,
I wandered far
Worshiping lower forms of creation.
I am done with that lower worship.
Through many of your lesser forms have I looked to find You
Yet each falls short of revealing Your Glory.
In fevered pitch, desire nature has sought You without,
Now I turn inward to find You alone.
Many incarnations have I wandered in darkness
Never knowing Your Light.
I demand you give me pure love for Thee,
I reject all outward forms
And call upon You to reveal Yourself.
Come to me, and make me know Your true Self
Absorb the little me until all I know is You, Eternal You.

O Infinite Light

O Infinite Light
You are all compassion seeking to awaken Your children,
Most seem to prefer dream-sleep
But here and there You stir some to wakefulness,
You touch Whom You will
None can anticipate Your moves,
But we ask, "Why do you not awaken all?"
For knowledge of You
Brings with it all joy and freedom from sorrow.
So, my Dear, awaken all from their false dreams
Remind them that they are lions of realization
Not bleating sheep of fear and desire.

Make Me Free in Thee

O Divine Mother
You have given me desire-nature
By the power of your Prakriti
I have entered the net of Maya.

O Divine Mother
We are told, in order to have freedom
We must be free from desire
Yet you have made me this way.

O Divine Mother
I look for completeness outside of me
I seek pleasure and satisfaction
In this world with five seductions.

O Divine Mother
You created me with this desire
Yet desire keeps me from knowing
Your vast infinite Self.

O Divine Mother
I pray deeply to You
Release me from this false desire
Make me free in Thee.

O Divine Mother
By the same power you made me
With desire for your Maya
Do it now! Make me One with You.

Your Child Nityananda

Oh Lord, may your child Nityananda,
Come to realize your eternal Presence
As love, bliss and light.
Watch over him, as I know you do.
Om Tat Sat

Your Child

Oh Lord, take care of your child
See that he sees his path straight
As Baba said, Bhakti is crying for God,
May your child, Nityananda
Open his heart to your unfathomable love and compassion.
Om Sri Ram Jai Ram Jai Jai Ram

O Joy Inexpressible

O Joy inexpressible
Dance with me
Make me move according to Thy rhythm,
You are moving through every cell of my being.
Each and every person is but Your attribute,
Nay, they can be but shadowy reflections.
Burn brightly O Joy!
Illumine the world
So that all creation
May move in concert with Thee alone!
Victory to sadhana
Victory to realization!

Prayer for Light

May the Light of God be ever:
In front of you to guide your way
Beneath your feet to support you
Behind you to give you strength
Beside you as your Friend of friends
Above to uplift your spirit
Within you to give you peace.

May the Light of God be ever:
In front of me to guide my way
Beneath my feet to support me
Behind me to give me strength
Beside me as my Friend of friends
Above me to uplift my spirit
Within me to give me peace.

I Know We Are One

Dear Divine Mother,
You are the comfort I seek
You accept me into your warm Being
In Union we reside, one with another,
Love manifests between us
And in You I know we are one.

O Heavenly Father
You are the shelter I seek,
Your strength is my surety
And Your blazing Light guides my way,
In Your tender touch, I know we are one.

O Creator of My Heart's Desire

O Creator of my heart's desire
Make my desire for Thee alone,
Since You have given me eyes
Let them search for You only.

In my hearing
The ring of creative Om,
On my tongue
The sweetness of amrita.

O Maker of all that is
Make me one with Thee,
In my heart You work continuously
Let it open in love for all.

I breathe in rhythm to life
Let it be sacred Kriya,
For pleasure I seek
In You I find Bliss sublime.

O Creator of my heart's desire,
Make me one with Thee.
It is You who created separation
End Thy game and make us One.

Absorbed

All life rises to the top
A beautiful pearl colored Light appears
O Lord reveal Thyself, reveal Thyself
Alone I await on You.

Absorbed in sweet contemplation
With still breath,
Alone I await on You
O please come to me my Lord.

Your all-powerful inner force
Draws me to ever-illumined spheres,
Purifying the cells of my Being
O Lord reveal Thyself, reveal Thyself.

Ever onward You call to me
All the earth stops,
Humble in awe
Alone, I await on You alone.

O Mighty Supreme Spirit

O Mighty Supreme Spirit
I pray that all souls may
Manifest Thy Light and Purity,
O Omnipotent force
You have created all,
Awaken Thy children
So that all may live in harmony
With Thy perfect will of peace and joy.

Make Me Know Thee

O Tender Lord
I know Thee only
I want Thee only
Fill my mind
Fill my heart
Make me know Thee
Make Thy Self manifest in me.
Not a sophisticated
Not an intellectual
But a Lover of Thee.
A lowly servant of Thee
You are my Goal
You are my Life
Let Your light shine.
Let Wisdom ring.
Be Thou my Lord
Make me Thine Instrument,
Brush away all debris
Burn out all dross.
Only Thee do I want
Only Thee do I seek
Make me one with Thee.
O Lord, make me Thine alone.

Four-Fold Blessing

Lord, bless me in four ways:
Let me serve Thee in all that I do.
Let me Love Thee in all whom I meet.
Let me discern Thee in all that I think.
And Lord, Let me strive for Thee alone in all that I practice.

Prayer for World Enlightenment

O Infinite Light of God
You are the indwelling Presence
Within all creation
Both animate and inanimate.

We pray to You
For the eradication of
All conflicts and fights
Both within and without.

We charge You with the responsibility of
Leading all Humankind.
Both individually, and collectively,
To live in harmony with their highest Light.

O Beloved indwelling Presence
You see to it
That dharma—right action
Is established on earth.

And that through right behavior
Corresponding to natural and Spiritual Law
Peace will reign supreme
And all Humankind will be uplifted
To your highest Light.
Om Peace Bliss Amen

Thou and I

O Heavenly Father
Delay no longer
Come to me
Comfort me
And make me know
Thou and I are ever One.

Be My Guide

Be My Guide
O Lord, guide Thou my thoughts
Make them anchored in Thee.

Guide Thou my feelings
Purify them for love of Thee alone.

Guide Thou my actions
To be in service to Thee always.

Guide Thou my words
Projecting Beauty, Truth and Thy vibration.

O Lord, guide me always, move through me,
Make me a perfect Instrument of Divine Will.

Prayer provides solace and ignites the inner fire. David shares a few of his heartfelt prayers and with each prayer he invites us to step deeper into our sacred, eternal soul-force.

In *My Spiritual India*, David shares Yogacharya Mother Hamilton's wisdom and affirms that the price of such seeking is to gain both the capacity for greater love and a glorious state of divinity.

> The search for the Self is the most thrilling adventure ever embarked upon by man because it covers every facet of life, both human and divine. It has been said that God-realization is the pearl of great price, but few there are who are willing to pay that price because they are afraid it will require of them more than they are willing to give. They are fearful that if they attain the state of Nirvana, or the Absolute, they will lose their identities, their individualities and personalities and become like the "salt doll," who went into the ocean to find out what it was like but melted before she could return to tell of the experience.

> I ask the question: "Have Krishna, Buddha, Jesus Christ, Mohammed, Zoroaster, Nanak and, in our own time, Ramakrishna, lost their identities? Are they not even today the greatest individuals with the greatest personalities who ever lived? And are they not still living in the hearts of men everywhere? Their names will be remembered long after all names cease to have any meaning. Why?" Because their love for God was greater than their love for themselves, because they had a greater vision of man's destiny and the courage and will to pay the price necessary to regain their lost paradise and to show the way that all must go if they are to attain the glorious state of divinity. *(pg. 339)*

David holds these great masters in his heart and through his Guru Tribute poems shows magnificent gratitude for those who have had the wisdom to answer the sacred Call and to forge the next evolutionary process for homo sapiens. The shared experiences and contribution to the human collective from these great masters has brought uncountable blessings to humanity as a whole and to the individuals who commit to the trek up the sacred mountain.

Top: Sri Yukteswar and Paramhansa Yogananda, India (circa 1935).
Below: Swamiji Satchidananda and Yogacharya David, Anandashram, India. 2002.

Chapter Six
Guru Tribute

David speaks frequently in his journals of his love for Krishna, Jesus, the Kriya Masters, Swami Ramdas, Mother Krishnabai (Mataji), Swami Satchidananda and other great spiritual men and women. He wrote poems offering tributes to a select group of masters as the muse of poetry directed him, especially to his Guru, Yogacharya Mother Hamilton. In his talks and retreats David spoke with reverence about many more great souls. These great Masters warrant a brief introduction placed in the context of David's words.

Krishna, as Mahavatar, standing above all lineage history held an important place in David's heart. He expresses some of this in *Tribute to Krishna*. The historical Krishna existed, his name is first mentioned in the *Chandogya Upanishad* where he was known as a spiritual teacher, avatar and a knower of Brahman. He was associated with the great epic *Mahabharata* and the immense battle, Kurukshetra, sometime from the 5th to the 1st century B.C. In the *Bhagavad Gita*, Krishna is presented as a divine Teacher supporting the spiritual illumination of the human being with the charge to destroy ignorance and falsehood and to bring divine knowledge back to the world. David had a strong loving connection with Krishna as you can discern through his poems *O Krishna my Heart, O Krishna,* and *O Krishna the One and the Many*. David also speaks to this deep connection in his year of silence in *Cloud Mountain Journals 2000–2001*.

David's poems *Guru is your Heart; Mother, Master, Saints and Sages All; God and Gurus; Maha,* concluding this initial tribute with *Through the Master* invokes the sacred Kriya lineage that was unique to David's point of view.

Jesus and Babaji are at the head of the Kriya lineage. According to the historical teachings as David tells it:

> Jesus requested that Babaji send a yogic master (Paramhansa Yogananda) to the West to re-awaken

original Christianity: the knowledge that the kingdom of heaven is within you, and there are means by which you may realize this great heaven of spiritual qualities while you yet live in a physical body. This kingdom of heaven is a universal experience; it will be the same for any person anywhere in the world, regardless of the individual's race, culture or religion. A God who is the Creator of all cannot but be the Father of all and therefore all are the children of the one, infinite, divine Source. Religions are many, but truth is one. Ultimate truth cannot be expressed in words; words are but reflections of real Truth. Therefore, scriptures are the author's best attempt to tell of the kingdom of heaven, an outer shell that indicates the fulfilling nut hidden inside.

This universal truth can be realized and there are many who have had glimpses of absolute truth, but very few have complete realization in its universal nature. Jesus took incarnation to teach the real nature of universal truth. Of his followers, there were a few who fully comprehended his meaning. Some partially received all that he came to reveal, and others missed much of what the spiritual Master came to teach. Down through the years many of the great truths and the means to realize these truths were distorted and/or deleted.

Since his incarnation, Jesus has continued to be a savior. He continues to bless and guide those who attune themselves to his Cosmic Consciousness. Like all truly realized masters, he communes with those who are also helping humanity to evolve. Babaji, the great Master of India, is also a Mahavatar, as is Jesus. A Mahavatar (a supreme avatar) is an avatar (descent of Spirit into flesh) who is pre-eminent over other spiritual masters; together Jesus and Babaji are working for the spiritual evolution of this world.

(Adapted from www.crossandlotus.com)

The teachings through many Kriya Masters speak of Master Jesus, in India sometimes spoken as Guru Issa, as the initiating spark for this Kriya lineage as he charged Babaji with the mission to reactivate the ancient sacred and hidden teachings of Light and Truth. Jesus, like Babaji, and other great masters has been known to appear to devotees.

At his Loon Lake Retreat in 2015, David spoke of Yogananda seeing Jesus four times, and understanding Jesus to be a 'living God.' Mother Hamilton in her devotion to Jesus, as David tells it, spoke of Jesus' love for God being so great that he is crucified on his own cross, which she says is his own body, in order that he may rise above the human condition to truly become the Christed One.

And Mother Hamilton says Jesus is right here guiding, leading and directing through that still small voice we call our soul. In the earlier poem *The Shepherd's Watch* we hear of Jesus' birth, in many other poems when we hear 'O Lord,' David is referring to Jesus as Lord or the Christ. Here in *Awake My Infinite Children*, David clearly wants to show us our infinite nature, our glorious crown, and the awaiting spiritual stairway.

David pays dedicated homage to Sri Sri Mahavatar Babaji who activated the Kriya Yoga lineage. Sri Mahavatar Babaji, meaning Great Avatar, met Lahiri Mahasaya around 1861. This amazing Avatar has been seen by Yogananda as described in his book *Autobiography of a Yogi,* by Sri Yukteswariji in his book *The Holy Science*, and he communicated with Yogacharya David during his Cloud Mountain retreat.

According to Yogananda's autobiography, Babaji has lived for hundreds of years in a remote region of the Himalayas of India and has been seen by only a few over the years. In *O Infinite Babaji,* David tells us that he feels Babaji's beloved presence "as the days of my life unfold" and in *Thank you Babaji* David fully places himself in Babaji's hands "Now and forever."

Lahiri Mahasaya (1828–1885) was the first disciple of Sri Sri Mahavatar Babaji from Varanasi, India. In a lecture titled *Lahiri Mahasaya: Father of Kriya Yoga*, at a retreat at Loon Lake in Canada, David shared Paramhansa Yogananda's statement:

Lahiri Mahasaya is a spiritual Master of the highest order. He was chosen by Babaji to bring Kriya Yoga to a new age. The Master was a householder yogi—that is he had a home, a wife, and children and worked at a job for many years until he retired; even then he took a job as a tutor in order to meet expenses. While meeting all the demands of a householder this greatest of spiritual masters practiced deepest meditation—fully exploring the inner world of a yogi.

David went on to say, as noted in the *Autobiography of a Yogi*: By the standards of both qualitative and quantitative good, the great master elevated the spiritual level of society. In his power to raise his close disciples to Christlike stature and his wide dissemination of truth among the masses, Lahiri Mahasaya ranks among the saviors of mankind. His uniqueness as a prophet lies in his practical stress on a definite method, Kriya, opening for the first time the doors of yoga freedom to all.

In *Beloved Baba* and in *Baba*, David shares how Lahiri Mahasaya comes to him through inner vision and David senses Lahiri Baba as an inner guide and great protector. About his poem, *Baba*, David writes:

This poem came to me after a visit to Lahiri Mahasaya's samadhi (place where the cremated ashes of his body reside) in holy Haridwar. Upon arriving on Holi Day, a sacred puja was being performed to Lahiri Mahasaya's samadhi site. After the puja we were given sacred leaves and then wandered the grounds. A smiling swami insisted we share in a feast. We sat on the ground under a rudraksha tree planted by Babaji. On leaf plates we were served a wonderful meal of fried chapatis, vegetable and chick pea sauce. Then Sweet Jubilees (grapes) were given for dessert. We felt the vibrations of the sacred trees of that place, and received rudraksha seeds from the ashram swami. His eyes were sparking, radiant with inner light. We were then ushered in to see a famous guru visiting from Rajasthan. This all brought to mind how three years ago we arrived at the same ashram. Unknown to us, we arrived on Lahiri Mahasaya's Mahasamadhi day. A group of devotees were meditating there and made us most welcome.

Although David spoke much of Sri Yukteswar (1885–1936), no poems were found specific to this great Master. With that in mind, and to give the reader a sense of Sri Yukteswar, included here is a brief quote from the *Autobiography of a Yogi*, included in David's talk, *A Meditation Upon the Life of a Great Master: Sri Yukteswariji*.

Yogananda asked Sri Yukteswar to speak about himself, Sri Yukteswar responds: "My family name was Priya Nath Karar. I was born here in Serampore, where father was a wealthy businessman. He left me this ancestral mansion, now my hermitage. My formal schooling was little; I found it slow and shallow. In early manhood, I undertook the responsibilities of a householder, and have one daughter, now married. My middle life was blessed with the guidance of Lahiri Mahasaya. After my wife died, I joined the Swami Order and received the new name of Sri Yukteswar Giri. Such are my simple annals." Yogananda states: "Master smiled at my eager face. Like all biographical sketches, his words had given the outward facts without revealing the inner man."

Another brief insight into the character of Sri Yukteswariji from the *Autobiograpy of a Yogi*:

When Sri Yukteswar was asked about Master Jesus. he responded: "The great masters of India mold their lives by the same godly ideals which animated Jesus; these men are his proclaimed kin: 'Whosoever shall do the will of my Father which is in heaven, the same is my brother, and sister, and mother.' 'If ye continue in my word,' Christ pointed out, 'then are ye my disciples indeed; and ye shall know the truth, and the truth shall make you free.' Freemen all, lords of themselves, the Yogi-Christs of India are part of the immortal fraternity: those who have attained a liberating knowledge of the One Father."

Next in David's tribute to the lineage comes a poem to Paramhansa Yogananda (1893–1952), fondly called Master by his disciples.
Master " . . . was the first yoga master of India whose mission it was to live and teach in the West. In the 1920's as he criss-crossed the United States on what he called "spiritual campaigns" his enthusiastic audiences filled large halls in America . . . He helped launch a spiritual revolution in the West." Yogananda felt that Kriya Yoga would ultimately spread in all lands harmonizing nations through a transcendental perception, through the ability of the human to "tear the veil of maya . . . to pierce the secret of creation through attaining a high interior state nirbikalpa samadhi . . . or through other practices such as the Word or Om, the divine sound."

David honored the original writings of Yogananda and saw him, as he states in *Our Beautiful Master*, arriving with "ancient oriental wisdom . . . bearing a universal message."

David wrote many poetic tributes to The Reverend Mother Yogacharya Mildred Hamilton (1904–1991). She was a direct disciple of Paramhansa Yogananda, whom she reverently called *Master*. Mother met Master in the year 1925. Her love and devotion to Master was unqualified as her lifelong Guru. Master healed Mother and her children of several serious illnesses. Master made Mother a minister in 1950, adding to her duties of Center Leader in Seattle. He also gave her direct permission to initiate others into Kriya Yoga, and later gave her the unique distinction as the only woman Yogacharya in his world-wide organization, and only one of seven in total. Mother once said she was the product of two fully realized Masters.

After the passing of her Guru, Mother received inner direction to go to India. There, in an ashram in the South of India, Swami

Ramdas, put Mother through the Mystical Crucifixion. As mentioned earlier, through these intense crucifixion experiences, the *New Testament* scriptures' inner meanings were revealed to her. Hidden beneath the outward story of Jesus was the story of what every human goes through in the ascent from the human to the Divine. This is Mother's unique contribution to the fund of world knowledge. Mother's love and service to God and Guru was complete and she was a blessing to all who knew her. In *Mother is my Master* we feel David's love for Mother Hamilton and his dire request to be delivered from "our terrible prison." And we see in *Mother's Cross* that David knew Mother Hamilton had paid the price that comes with realization. In *Om Mother, Mothers Day, Bless Mother Tonight*, and *Behold Divine Mother* we sense the human and the divine layer upon layer infinitely testing, gifting and offering Grace.

David begins his *Tribute to Swami Ramdas* (1884–1963) with a poem from his journal that was written by Swami Ramdas himself. Swami Ramdas or Beloved Papa as he was known by devotees around the world, was said to have enjoyed an extraordinary intimate relationship with God, whom he addressed as Ram. Born Vittal Rao, he was initiated in 1920 by his father into the Gurumantra RAMNAM. Shortly after, continued repetitions led to Vittal renouncing family life and following his Ram-call to wander India under inner sacred direction. After many years of wandering and time spent in caves, he was now called Swami Ramdas. With his senior devotee, Mother Krishnabai, he founded Anandashram near Kanhangad in Kerala State, South India. Their aim was to bring Universal Love and Service to the world. Soon they were endearingly called Papa and Mataji. Ramdas was clear that he did not belong to any particular creed as he believed all spiritually worthy creeds, religions and faiths are different paths which ultimately lead to the same goal—all are from "the first eternal cause of all existence."

Mother Hamilton first met Papa, not in India, but at his hotel in Seattle, Washington, while he was on his world tour in 1954. At a Loon Lake retreat, David relayed Mother's account of this meeting, described in an article published in *The Vision*, in 1968. She said:

He invited me to be seated and we sat and talked for a

while, exchangingt our views on God and His Truth. I then asked if we might meditate together, not realizing that for one who had already attained there was no need to meditate. He and his Father were already one. However, he said sweetly, 'Yes, let us meditate.' So, I sat at his feet and immediately felt myself lifted up into the Presence of God. What peace, what joy, what bliss I experienced. He said afterwards that I had left body-consciousness. I do not know. It was an indescribable experience. Little did I dream then that my meeting with him was to change the whole course of my life, in order that I might fulfill my destiny.

About the poem *Love's Ways are Strange* by Swami Ramdas, David says:

Papa's poem is both wonderful and terrible; for it contains the totality of life in its verses. God is the love (described), and love is God; this is absolutely true. You face God daily in the life that you lead. For the pragmatist, God comes in the form of practical solutions to life's vexing problems; to the mystic, life is a constant expression of Divine Life; to the depressed, life is living in a small dark cave; to the one 'in love,' God is walking on air. For each one lives on the same planet, but in a different world. You determine the world you live in by what you focus your mind upon. Think of yourself as separate, apart, and alone, and you are. Think of yourself as connected to the Infinite Being, surrender yourself to it, and you become one with God.

Love and God are exactly as Papa describes. It is the mind that determines that only when you have what you deem good do you feel happy, and when you experience what you judge to be bad do you doubt. Mother always taught, "Keep your mind on God," knowing that what you constantly fill your mind with is what you become. So, my friends, what do you wish to become?

When Krishna revealed his universal form to Arjuna, it was awe-inspiring and eventually became overwhelming; Arjuna was not yet ready to remain in the universal vision. You must surrender all that you think you understand about life at the feet of the Infinite, good and bad, high and low, and become totally open to the mind of God. It is then the mirror of your mind may be so perfectly clear that it reflects only your Divine Nature; only then may you be truly free!

As is evident from David's tribute poems to Swami Ramdas, David saw Papa as this cheery, child-like, powerful all-pervading presence who is filled with bliss no matter what befalls, each poem brings out an aspect of these traits: *Papa's Presence, Papa All-Pervading Presence,* and *O Infinite Papa.*

David follows the Tribute to Swami Ramdas with his *Tribute to Mataji.* Mother Krishnabai (1903–1989) known as Mataji, met Papa in 1928 after her husband passed away. She became Papa's foremost disciple. She attained Self-realization—Universal Vision and was instrumental in the development of Anandashram through her loving service to Papa and all who sought spiritual guidance. To David, Mataji epitomized the Divine Mother and in his poem *O Mataji* he clearly acknowledges the grace and power of the divine Shakti.

Swami Satchidananda receives David's tribute as well. Swami Satchidananda (1919–2008) met Papa Ramdas in 1947 when he came to Anandashram for a short visit. He was captured by the inner light and call to his spirit. Within a year or two he returned, never to leave. He served Swami Ramdas and Mother Krishnabai for over 30 years, traveling the world with them and documenting detailed conversations shared in *The Gospel of Swami Ramdas.* Swamiji become the Swami Guardian over Anandashram when Papa and Mataji left the body.

About the poem, *Swamiji's Grace,* David says:
> Written on the eve of our departure from Anandashram, my heart poured itself out in these words. I had told Swamiji, in my pilgrimage three years ago, that I felt

he was my second spiritual Mother, after Mother Hamilton. What words can describe the overwhelming love and gratitude I have for this great God-man? Perhaps you will taste that feeling through these picture-words. When we left Anandashram it was the day after Shivarati. The ashram had had celebrations of music and talks until midnight. Our taxi left at 2:30 am. Swamiji and other friends were up to lovingly send us off. I gave Swamiji a copy of this poem at that time, having read it to him at an earlier time. When I gave it to him at this pre-dawn goodbye—he rolled it up and made it look like he was putting a feather in his cap, perhaps the peacock feather Krishna wears in his crown.

The poems *Swamiji* and *Swamiji's Grace* ring out with David's love and respect for Swamiji, and more, he clearly states that Swamiji is his Second Mother, the mother he required to tenderly bring him to full God-realization.

We conclude this chapter with a poem to Anandamayi Ma (1896–1982). Her name was translated by Yogananda to mean 'Joy-Permeated.' Known for her precognition and healings "she was the embodiment of a joyous self-sufficiency, which enraptured the hearts of all who came near her." About his poem, *Ma*, David notes:

Ma was written after arriving in Kukhul, just outside Hardiwar. We went to Ma's samadhi temple where they were performing arati. Previous to this visit, I felt Ma's guiding presence take us to Almora and Dhaulchina, two ashrams dedicated to Anandamayi Ma. Dhaulchina provided the atmosphere for deepened sadhana and beautiful vistas. The simplicity of the ashram, built up around Swami Nirgunananda, made a perfect haven for peace for the inner opening of the heart of our three sadhakas. When after seven days, we returned to Almora, the sincere Brahmacharya Maharaj, unlocked Ma's bedroom upon my request. The vibrancy of the room made the heart soar in supernal realms. The overnight train brought us to the feet of Ma's samadhi temple. The morning arati was just beginning. It is an elaborate arati that lasts for some time. I soon became absorbed in Ma's Presence that lasted nearly the entire time. I remained seated. I came to know later, during the arati about the bringing of the light for all to take. However, the inner absorption transcended the outer ritual, perhaps to the discomfort of others. Jai Ma! Victory to the Universal Divine Mother.

With this brief context complete, supplemented by David's heart-felt sharing on how some of these poems were birthed, enjoy the wonder of David's gratitude and his delight that in this wondrous and mysterious universe, planet earth can be gifted with individuals graced with truth consciousness and unsurmountable wisdom.

Tribute to Krishna

O Krishna in My Heart

O Krishna in my heart,
Playful and joking is your art.
How you beguile every devotee,
With all the joy you let us see.

Of your sports do we see,
Your frolicking laughter to set us free.
I can see you now in nature's field,
Giving of your gifts in great yield.

Now and then do we lose our sight,
When our mind takes off in flight.
But then we suffer cruel duality,
And soon we forget how to Be.

We laugh and then cry,
We lose our breath and then sigh.
We think we're powerful and then weak,
One moment we think we know all and the next we seek.

How far we stray from oneness state,
How far we lose sight of our fate.
Soon our tears are running full,
We feel your heartstrings begin to pull.

Then begins to dawn your personal Light,
Our Spiritual Wings begin to take flight.
How I Love your Supreme Presence,
Loving You is my only Pretense.

Fill us up with your Self,
Make us strong in your Self.
Wisdom overflows in Thy presence,
Love is all in all with your glance.

O Krishna

O Krishna, my blue-colored Christ
See thy child in this form
And deign to grant me this boon
That I might know Thee truly.

It is You, O Krishna
Who has made me as I am,
It is You, O Hari
Who has stolen my heart.

It is You, O eternal Spirit
Who has given me dual nature,
And it is You my beloved
Who must resolve the many into One.

O my beautiful Celestial One,
Make me one with your Self,
Absorb the little me in to the great I Am
Forever and ever more.

O Krishna the One and the Many

O Krishna my heart
O Krishna my love
I am slain in spirit
By Your arrow of love.

My heart aches in sweet ecstasy
And opens as a bursting seed
Reaching for its beloved light
Full of life and promise.

A love without beginning
A love without end
A love without cause
A love without effect.

Perfect
Complete
Total
And One

Such is my love
Yet not my love
But Thy love
You who has become me.

The many become two
Two become One
One and Two are the many
The many are really One.

O maddening words get in the way
Of what I yearn to express,
The seed bursts and gushes forth
With promise of new weed.

Is there receptive ground?
Who is willing to prepare for it?

Who will die in order to live?
Who will yield in self mastery?

O blessed Infinite Beloved
Who has borne me with purpose
Creating vast potential but from a grain
Fulfill Thy Will in me.

Make me mad with love for Thee
Make me see Thee
As my all in all
Make me know Thee alone, Thee alone!

Tribute to David's Kriya Lineage

Mother, Master, Saints and Sages All

O Mother, Master, saints and sages all,
You hold a mirror to my soul.
"Come! Behold your Self in Me,"
You proclaim,
"Envision Your true Being."

O Mother, Master, saints and sages all,
My mirror darkened,
My doors to the soul are rusty,
And the cells of my Being are spiritually dead.

O Mother, Master, saints and sages all,
Open these blind eyes to Your Light,
Swing wide the gates to Heavenly Realms,
Awaken this sleeper to Your all-encompassing Spirit!

O Mother, Master, saints and sages all,
You are not vague and far off,
But deep, profound—the core of Truth.
Verily, You are my Self, ever calling me.

Guru is Your Heart

Guru is your heart. Guru is the glorious Light of God.
Guru is sown into every part of creation. Guru is savior of humankind.
Through the Light of Guru darkness is dispelled.
Guru is universal, without beginning or end.
See the blazing Light of the Guru!
Know ye not you are made in Its likeness of Spirit
It inhabits your image of three bodies.
Guru is Love. Guru is Light. Guru is Wisdom.
Guru is power of Yoga.
Guru is not man, woman, nor any one person or thing.
Guru is savior to all creation.
Guru uses man, woman or any vehicle It chooses
To awaken darkened souls in ignorance
To enlighten Souls of Realization.
As loving as mother and father is Guru.
As desirous for union as newly wed couple is Guru
To be in union with their beloved devotee,
Union not of bodies, but of hearts, minds and souls.
Union of Universal Consciousness.
Union to the union of all unions.
O glorious and ecstatic Guru,
In form or formlessness
It burns ever within you and all about you.
O sadhaka, purify your eyes so you may see Guru-glory.
Make your eye of attention so you may see Guru-Light.
Quiet the mind so you may hear Its entrancing voice.
Guru is nigh to you now.
Wait no longer but find your Guru now, now ever more.

Maha

Om Mother: Bless me with love for God, a love so strong that i pass through every test, endure any hardship in my ascendancy to Sahaja Oneness with my Infinite Beloved.

Om Master Paramhansa Yogananda: Bless me with deepening meditation bliss. Absorb body and mind into the omnipotent almighty Supreme Being.

Om Sri Yukteswar: Grant me wisdom to discern Truth from falsehood. Open my eye of wisdom to pierce into the true nature of all things. Give me a calm mind to be perfectly attuned to Divinity Itself.

Om Lahiri Mahasaya: Guide me my Baba into Kriya practice to plumb the depths of Spirit. Bless me to be absorbed into the spinal and brain centers, opening the sacred channels of divine absorption.

Om Mahavatar Babaji: Absorb me into thy great Being of All-Encompassing Spirit. Free me from every limitation and guide me into everlasting freedom in God.

Om Jesus: Bless Me, O Divine Master, with perfect Love for God and complete surrender to His Will. Lead me into his eternal Kingdom of Spirit; until there is only One, only One.

Om Papa: Reveal to me the Universal Vision in which I see only God's Light and God's Will in all people, all things, all situations. Teach me to lift the mask of maya and know it is the Divine Mother playing every role, to find God laughing and playing at each bend in the road.

Om Mataji: Make me fearless to serve God in everyone I meet; to speak the truth, always, to spend my life in service to God and Guru without reserve.

Om Swamiji: Teach me to be never complacent about knowing or serving God. Prompt me always to dive deeper, soar higher. Make me have that quality common to all men and women of divine realization, pleasing to God above all other qualities: humility.

God and Gurus

O Babaji, Mother and All,
Bless me, that Perfection
Manifests within and without.
Work Thy will through me,
And may all be done
For the highest good of all.
Om Peace Bliss Amen.

Through the Master

Through the Master
The servant is given access to all.
The servant lives in a mansion,
He travels the world,
And has useful work,
All due to being under
The Grace of His Master.

He may meet the great of the greats,
Most humble in circumstances
All his world, all his experiences come from his Master
And in this he is content, well satisfied.

Tribute to Jesus as Yogi

Awake My Infinite Children

On this glorious morn
In day of ancient yore
Awoke a sleeping Christ
And arose through that infinite door.

"Arise my sleeping beauties
Awake from your sleeping state"
He called to his beloved ones then,
And His echo stays with us now.

Can history give record to that wonderful day
When man transcended this world
And joined his final fate
Of finding the Heavenly Kingdom for all time?

"O wake you sleeping children,
Wake to yonder dawn
Hear that distant horn
That calls you from your sleep."

Who can say of our waking Nature
Who can say who we truly are,
When darkness and sleep
As a shroud o'er our deadened form hangs about?

Can letters or books tell us,
Or another with beautiful words
Inform us of that wonder
Calling us from unbidden realms?

"O wake my infinite children
Forsake your sleep once and for all,
Awake from dark consciousness
And know the unfolding dawn."

The shroud has lifted its veil
To reveal that subtler Nature
To which we have all been called
A Nature that ever will be ours.

"O wake my infinite children,
Hear that distant horn,
Know you are God's child
And one with that infinite Sound."

O so many years ago
On such an Easter morn
Awoke the sleeping Christ
Never to sleep again.

Who would have thought to dream
On that day of old
That two millennia in future
We would hear that message clear.

"O wake my infinite child,
Forsake your sleep of the night
Awake to your infinite Nature
And know your glorious crown.
Ascend your spiritual stairway,
Each flower unfolding,
Each mystery unwound,
Every truth revealed before your inner vision."

"O awake my infinite children,
Awake to your ultimate fate,
Awake to your Infinite Nature
Awake to God's natural state."

Tribute to Sri Sri Mahavatar Babaji of the Kriya Yoga Lineage

O Infinite Babaji

O Infinite Babaji
Your Grace knows no bounds
You teach your most inept devotee
With such patience and love.

How can I say the gratitude I feel?
How can I show you my love?
How can I serve you with greater devotion?
Will you show me as the days of my life unfold?
Inwardly I see you smile and nod affirmatively.

Thank You Babaji

Thank You Babaji
For guiding our steps here,
For the thunderous Om
And all good things You bring to us,
Fulfill Your purpose in us, now!
We are in Your hands,
Now and forever!

Tribute to Lahiri Mahasaya

Beloved Baba

Sweet Lahiri Baba
What smile forms upon your lips?
What cosmic game do you play?
In sweet, kind gentleness you come.

O Baba!
You stand behind Earth's glaring Light,
And reside in subtler realms.
Through inner vision you come.

As supreme Master,
Humility clouds your greatness
Lost in common life of all that lives
You come to the humble in heart.

O spiritually illumined one,
You lived a life in hearth and house
Performed ordinary earthly tasks
You came to show us the golden middle way.

Blessed Baba
To sincere Kriya Bhaktas
Your perfumed essence exudes your presence
In sweet revelation on trails and ways.

Wonderful Master Baba
Awaken in me your cosmic vision
Show me your inner wealth
And come to me now!

BABA

Baba of my heart
How elusive you are
To come within my vision
Now you are ever-present.

Baba of my soul
You have given me
Numberless inner darshans
With power to awaken a slumbering soul.

Baba of sweet kindness
Your master and you are one.
You look so kindly after your spiritual son
And all who look trustingly to you.

Baba of thoughtfulness
Twice have I been to your samadhi
In holy Haridwar
Doorway to God.

You received me two times
With such graciousness
Arranging for sacred rites
And sacred feasts.

My cup runneth over
With blessings and ambrosia
Of Spiritual vibration
And human manifestation of kindness.

My Lahiri Baba
No stranger are you to me
But an inner guide
And powerful protector.

Once you were hard to find
But that is your lila
Once doors remained closed
But now they stand gracefully wide.
My blessed Baba
Eternal Guru of my heart and soul
You illumine me with a glance
And forever we are one.

Tribute to Paramhansa Yoganandaji

Our Beautiful Master

Our beautiful Master
With ancient oriented wisdom
Arrived on Western shores
A beatific Light for the ages.

He came bearing a universal message,
A God-inspired prophet
In a delightful human package
Wreathed in smiles and bliss.

O he charmed and amazed
Packed audiences from shore to shore,
An ambassador of Yogic tradition
Styled for embracement by all sincere seekers.

Our beautiful Master
We bow at your feet
For you have searched us out
Even as the sun burns through a smothering fog.

We bow at your feet
And we follow in your footsteps
That we may become—ever as you—
Ever One with our Infinite Beloved.

We bow at your feet
For being the Light in our darkness
And a guide to us in our confusion
O our beautiful Master.

Tribute to Yogacharya Mother Hamilton

Mother is My Master

Mother is my master, of this I know
She is with me everywhere I go.
Many the times in dire need,
She helps me by doing a mighty deed.

Smiling and tender is her natural way,
Warm and loving She fills my every day.
Stern and powerful when we're in harms way,
Loving again when at home we stay.

Wonderful she treats us, like children all,
Long does she work to give us God's call.
If we just once turn over the field,
Her mighty seed will give a great yield.

Receive the call of my Mother Divine,
For it is God's presence that we pine.
She will lead us back home again,
And free us forever from our terrible prison.

Mother's Day

O Heavenly Mother,
Shine on us your Love's cover.
On this day we bow to you,
You are God, of that we know.

Blow away our shadow's dark,
On us, put God's mark.
Hard you work to make us clear,
How easily you bring God near.

This is Mother's Day as you know,
Our love and devotion we wish to show.

But how do we say that which is deep in our heart,
Except by making ourselves God's part.

O Dear Mother on this day we wish,
For ourselves to be caught in your heart
Like a fish.
No one alive can tell us naught,
That Your very self is not God's thought.

But this is Your day as you know,
So let the Lord glorify your show.
Through every cell of you does God blow,
From your every thought, may God grow.

Mother's Cross

Through brilliant shining Light
Came Divine Mother in human guise,
Strong of Spirit and world wise
She bore the weight of human kind.

Through battles mighty and stringent tests
Our Divine Mother wore her crown
Of blazing Light from Human to Divine.

O Divine Mother, how you strove
To bring truth and grace in a clarion call,
Without reserve you gave your all
And made us know the Light within.

Both East and West lay open bare
To your intuitive wisdom gaze
And to one and all you shared your knowledge
Of myth's darkened maze
That passed as scripture of times before.

After paying the price for this truth and more
And crowned with glory by saints and devotees,

You took more of the world's disease
Into your three-tiered bodied cross.

The world
Is ignorance, pain and deprivation too,
You embraced and took into your self
And labored to purify that living hell
Of the world's misery and self-destructive tendency.

You dove deep into ignorance snare
Took the world's woe as your own,
And fought gallantly, with barely a moan,
Alone you struggled for Light's glory.

And having fought true, to the end of your strength
You died alone with barely a friend,
Deserted by many in a descending trend
You brought to this world an enduring example.

My dearest Mother, how I love you so
And all you have done for this world of ours,
How you suffered for us that we might dare
To cross delusions ocean and know your Light.

And now I find your Light in me
Your wisdom glimmering in my mind,
I now feel you standing close in bliss sublime
Your Glory uplifting my heart, mind and soul.

I now find you glowing in others
Through love and wisdom, peace Divine,
Your broken body of yore spread seeds of
A living spiritual kind
And new life is starting in many a new heart.

Let us with patience and persistence
That matches Mother's own
Strive for that Light alone
And lay ourselves at her feet forever and ever more.

OM MOTHER

Divine Mother of One and all
You have given us life and soul
And given all we may call our own.

Om Mother,
You have manifested as each one's mother,
Sometimes You are love manifest
And sometimes destroyer of Dreams.

Behind all manifestations
I see You in loving form
For all disguises You wear
Work for good, one and all.

Om sweet Mother,
I honor and lay my love
Upon your shining feet of gold
Leaving in surrender my good for all.

Om Mother
You manifest as all Mothers
Make me know it is You shining in all
Shine your sunlit love upon me now!

Om sweet Mother
I feel you close now
Your hand touches my outstretched hand
We are forever, forever one.

BLESS MOTHER TONIGHT

O Lord of Light
Haloed in blue
Bless Mother tonight.

Lift her up, squeeze her tight,
Answer my prayers true
Bless Mother tonight.

Her spirit is great, so much fight,
Her body cells renew
Bless Mother tonight.

O Lord of Heaven, Lord of Light
Pure as the morning dew,
Bless my Mother tonight.

O Lord of Light
Haloed in blue
Bless Mother tonight.

Lift her up, squeeze her tight
Answer my prayers true,
Bless Mother tonight.

Her spirit is great, so much fight
Her body cells renew,
Bless Mother tonight.

O Lord of Heaven, Lord of Light
Pure as the morning dew
Bless my Mother tonight.

Behold Divine Mother

Behold my Divine Mother,
Radiance, Wisdom and Love itself.
Like a Light in the dark,
Bringing Music to the deaf
And Color to the blind.

As we limp and use crutches to move,
Trying to walk the razor's edge,
Behold the Mother Divine beckoning us ever on.
How we struggle ever onward,
There she stands, like a Mother
Urging her child's first steps.

We often fall, sometimes very hard,
As we recover in sorrow and shame,
We look up to our Mother's Omnipresent Love.
She comes to us in such humility,
With her bewitching smile,
She changes us, never to be the same.

As the Master Gardener
She waters us with Love,
She removes our fruitless branches.
O Divine Mother, shine on us
Like the Sun to its tree,
Create in us the Son of God
You see all so clearly.

Behold my Divine Mother,
Radiance, Wisdom and Love itself.
Like a light in the dark,
Bringing Music to the deaf and
Color to the blind.
Om Sri Ram, Jai Ram

Tribute to Swami Ramdas

Love's Ways are Strange (by Swami Ramdas)

Love's ways are strange!
It is less than the least,
Greater than the greatest.
'Tis humble—'tis proud.
It yields as the reed in the wind,
It is firm like a rock unshaken.
'Tis soft as a flower,
Hard as adamant.
It is filled with bliss,
'Tis surcharged with sorrow.
'Tis gentle and smiling as the new-born babe,
'Tis stern and grim like a volcano.
'Tis kind—it is cruel,
It wants all—it wants nothing,
It creates—it destroys,
Love's ways are strange!

Papa

O Papa, be mine tonight!
Break through this darkened gloom
And fill my waiting soul
With your shining, radiant ecstasy.
O Papa, will you be mine tonight?
Say it will be so.
Lead me to your guiding Light
So that I may know you truly, now and forevermore.

Papa All-Pervading Presence

Papa, you are the all-pervading presence,
Like a doorway
Wide open to unending peace and joy
Hari Om, my beloved Papa.

O Infinite Papa

O Infinite Papa,
You have assumed each personality
For your immortal play.
You ask, "What's the fun?"
Is fun not a part of every living thing in space?
And is not every aspect filled with your ever-joyful life?
Verily, where are you not!

Tribute to Mother Krishnabai
(affectionately called Mataji)

O Mataji

O Mataji, an expression of the Divine Mother,
Continue to grace me with the power to purify this consciousness.
Leave no speck or blemish upon it.
It is by your grace and your power this work is done.
Make me see Thee in all.
Raise this Shakti to the heart center and beyond.
Jai Mataji, Jai Guru Jai Ram!

Tribute to Swami Satchidananda

Swamiji

Swamiji, gratitude swells my heart.
Tenderness touches the tiniest nerve endings.
Surrender lays me at your feet.
Peace is vibrant in the air and space.
You, who are my Second Mother,
With All-Consciousness you pervade me.
In simplicity your smile melts hardness,
And humor sparkles your eyes.
As gopis of ancient Bharat,
We dance drunkenly in full moon light,
And our greatest joy, our greatest joy,
Is to make you happy in the dance!
O Swamiji, love hangs as dew on a rose.
The heart knows no bounds
And rises into infinite expanse,
Then settles as golden dust at your feet.

Swamiji's Grace

A mystic shroud
Has beclouded my mind
Hiding the expression of clear words
To tell of Thy Grace.

It is a grace that flows
So sweetly and gentle
Lifting one so gradually
That the lifting can go unnoticed.

Other times it is
A Light that shines so greatly
So as to illumine the entire world
With sweetness and love Divine.

Those in need, approaching you
See you as the fount of prosperity
And many are the kinds of need
That you tend to in a constant giving.

Maybe the need for a home
Or a loan or gift of currency
Some clothes, food or travel funds
All flows from your giving heart.

Others are sick in body
Perhaps a heart that has been broken
By life's disappointments and calamities
Or the greatest illness: discouragement.

With wisdom and sweet solicitude
You pour a healing balm of medicine
Both visible and invisible
To all who come in such need.

There are others who come
For your greater gifts
Gifts without measure or adequate description
To ascertain their true worth.

Those are the gifts of Spirit
That naturally flow to receptive hearts
And bring solace to the weary
And strength to continue on.

Or, it may be direction to the bewildered
Courage to the faint of heart
Clarity to confused minds
And love to those parched of the same.

All this you do
With the outward ease of a child

As would the perfect craftsman
Make an impossible task look so easy.

All this you do
Without thought or desire
For what may come your way
As a result of being a fount of Grace.

"It is all Papa"
You will say with a twinkle
"All Papa" you say
But is it not Papa who has become you?

You are our beloved Swamiji
For me there is none other
You dwell in the hearts of one and all
Dwelling in my heart as well.

Perhaps a ray of Light
Has pierced that shroud
That hid from me the right words
To indicate what resides in you.

For that Light is shining brightly
Within the bosom of this heart
And wishes to express itself
In joyous gratitude of words.

The glory of that beautiful Light
I see so brilliant in your words and deeds
So gentle a flow of grace
Flowing for all to see.

A grace so strong and wide
To lift all receptive souls
And reclaim the paradise lost
And make us one with thee.

Tribute to Anandamayi Ma

O Ma

O Ma
Seated in samadhi mandir
Listening to sacred chants
Incense filling the air.

You take me in hand
Having guided me to your feet
And lift me gently to your Heavenly realm
Beyond the marble tomb.
You are the incarnation of love
Making the heart strong and sure
Filling it with premanand
Making it sing in Thy Presence.

The inward spine grows in magnitude
The body loses definition
The jaw grows slack
Breathing becomes nil.

Consciousness escapes body's frame
And floods out in unending peace,
Self resounds everywhere
Your grace is beyond measure.

Ariti's song goes by unnoticed,
Absorbed in your inner light
Outer form dissolves into one
Vast Light of peace and love.
O Ma!
How to tell of thy glory
Shared in a secret way?
How to bring that spell to all,
That delivers one at the Infinite's feet?

Love blossoms in the ready heart,
Wisdom grows in the surrendered mind,
Purity enters the empty vessel,
Freedom rings in the unfettered soul.

O Ma
You are The Divine Mother of all
O Ma
Make us sing thy glorious name evermore.

Gratitude pervades the *Guru Tribute* poems, and devotion. One senses David's profound thankfulness and sublime joy acknowledging that Masters exist, that the Divine exists, that there is a sublime reality of divine existence, and in knowing this to be true, David shares with us how deeply his heart opens and how it fills with a marvellous joy.

Now that you have a sense of how David experienced the greatness of India's masters, we turn to poems that speak to the beauty and mystical—*India's Gifts*.

Yogacharya Mother Hamilton (circa 1977).

Left: Lahiri Mahasaya, India. Right: Papa Ramdas, India. (circa 1960).

Ganges River at Dawn, Benares, India. 2005.

Chapter Seven
India's Gifts

David made several pilgrimages to India starting in 1998. Each trip brought David and those who accompanied him to Anandashram, the abode of Swami Ramdas, Mother Krishnabai and now Swami Satchidananda, who when he left his body passed the Swamiji spiritual mantle to Swami Muktananda.

Anandashram is the ashram where Yogacharya Mother Hamilton made her 1957–1958 pilgrimage after Paramhansa Yogananda left his body. Mother's intention was to stay until she had attained God-realization. Under Swami Ramdas and Mother Krishnabai's spiritual care, Mother went through an intense and transformative spiritual experience, a "Mystical Crucifixion." Mother Hamilton attained the God-realization she sought.

India brought many gifts to David. He shares some of these gifts through poems and prayers, as well as his tribute to the Masters and accounts of personal experiences in his journals. Here we share poems that address specific aspects of his pilgrimages and poems that offer grand images of the mountains and their role in spiritual sadhana.

We start with David's 2005 pilgrimage to India and Anandashram, where David describes the morning Flower Ceremony. There are five prayers for five stations, and David describes his prayers.

Poems written at various times are preceded by David's journal writings which give context to David's experience of "Holy India" and the ageless spirit of its soul.

Anandashram Flower Ceremony

Each morning in the Flower Ceremony we enter the Meditation Hall or Bhajan Hall. There in the inner sanctum are five stations that I bow to. A separate prayer at each station issues from my mind.

The first station is a lighted lamp in a glass box:
"O Purusha (Light of my Being)
Ever illuminate my Ajna."

Next is a round Lotus carving:
"O Sahaswara realization—
Open fully the petals of Thy
Infinite realization."

Then Papa's bones stored in a box of marble:
"May You so saturate my being and body,
That your purity will
Permeate the very bones of my body."

I come next to the carved lotus with Papa's feet in the middle:
"O Purushottama
May I be Thy full manifestation."

Finally, Mataji's feet in the carved lotus:
"O Mataji, bless me that
I render perfect service
With body, heart, mind and soul."

With Swami Sachidananda kindly welcoming all who enter the Mandir and offering flowers to each ripe soul, the morning continues. David shares a poem in gratitude to Swamiji the careful loving guardian of the Ceremony.

O Swamiji

O Swamiji
Darling of our hearts
You draw our attention
To God and Gurus alone.
Your selfless service
Purifies the world
And makes us clean
In Infinite Love.
Hari Om!

The Mandirs

The Mandirs are samadhi temples built over the place where Papa Ramdas and Mataji's bodies were cremated. Ram Nam means God's name. Ram Nam is singing God's name as mantra, repeated again and again with deepened absorption in the vibration of the name.

Each morning around 5:30 a.m., the Mandir is opened and the 12 hours of continuous Ram Nam begins. The men begin the day's chanting, then the women take over at 6:30, then they alternate all through the day. This early morning is one of my favorite times of chanting. One morning, after chanting, I felt the urge to write about my experience. The image of sailing ships had come spontaneously to mind that very morning, and the intoxication of expanded consciousness was very present.

Mandir's Freedom

Walking about sacred ashes
Singing God's sweetness
Repeating His Nam again and again
I enter into the realm of name.

The doors resist opening
But with a push through
I enter in and feel the difference
Into the Infinite realm.

I feel lighter in body at first,
A thrill goes up my spine,
Consciousness expands
Blissful joy plays through the body cells.

A feeling-picture makes me think
We are so many ships circling about
With Masts of spines rising tall
Majestic movement glides round and round.

O Bliss-filled motion moves
In gentle rhythm
And walls, floor and ceiling
Expand without limit
To all space, beyond time.

Like ink dropped in still water
It expands and dissolves
Not into nothingness
But into the Allness of infinitude.

Body is but a drop
In that Infinite Sea,
An ocean realm of peaceful Joy
Consciousness, set free at last!

"O Grace of Nam and sacred ash
Set this world free in Thee,
Let all mankind and every speck of dust
Know of Your eternal freedom."

"Let all become graceful ships
Sailing upon ocean's Bliss
Knowing freedom in Truth
And purity in Thee."

CALLED BACK TO INDIA

Now in 2001, after three years, I have been called back to India. The last trip was full of sadhana and peak spiritual experiences. Since that time sadhana deepened still more, a year of silence and solitude during which something very deep stabilized. Now I stand on rock, no more shifting sand. This is reflected in my experience in returning to India. Before I remained in solitude, only moving out to seek darshan with Swamiji daily. Now others seek me out, without any effort of my own, for spiritual counsel and inspiration. I witness the change, without moving from the rock. My role has shifted, my Beloved is eternally the same. The *Song Eternal* is an expression of my current state.

Song Eternal

O Infinite, eternal Beloved
You reside so deep within my soul,
Like a little wave You play on the surface of my awareness
Then deep, like a sounding Boom
You resound in the Infinite depths.
Fortunate are those who hear your symphony
Making holy all who have ears to hear You.
In joyful humility one listens and
Nay! Becomes Your Blissful resonance.
You madden the soul with Divine love.
You speak a prayer through my listening mind:
O my beloved, forsake me never!
Is it I who speaks that prayer to You,
Or is it You who speaks it to me?
I cannot discern the difference.
For in that holy Spirit
That inner sanctum sanctorum
There is a blending of soul and Spirit,
One becomes the other, without clear
Definition of one from another
With only love, light and oneness
Ever calling its song to all!

In Silence

Written at Anandashram. It came to me spontaneously, as all the writings have. However, unlike some of the other poems, this one did not have its direct inspiration from any event of the time. Rather, I felt it come from the deep well-springs of experience of my year in silence. The conscious and superconscious experience of that yet seemed to well-up in the words of this poem.

Silence

Silence is Stillness,
Stillness of body, speech, thought,
All comes into a quiet
Quietness becomes stillness.

No past intrudes here,
No future stretches ahead,
Only the present
In all of its fullness.

If activity survives,
It only plays on the surface
And leaves the vast ocean
Unaffected in its depth.

Being replaces doing,
Awareness is absent of thinking,
Stillness is eloquent
And denotes silence.

All the worlds come
From this potent Stillness,
And they reside in it
But stillness is not contained by the worlds.

It comes with practice
But as a spontaneity

Of its own making
We can be its servant,
But not its master.

Be still,
And know that I AM God
Be quiet,
And know the I AM of your Being.

And in the I AM
Know you are forever one
With the Eternal
Without Beginning or End.

Be still
Enter into quiet
Become one
In the silence of your soul.

Grant my One Request

I have come from distant shores,
Following yonder star
To the ancient land Bharat;
I seek the One alone worth finding.

O Infinite Mother of grace,
Will you not grant me my one request,
To gain the Universal Vision of Your great being,
To be established in eternal Oneness with You.
Om Tat Sat.

CRUSHING OF THE 'OLD CUP'

Written at Anandashram as Carla was going through intensive experiences of the mystical crucifixion. The depth of these experiences and their effect on us cannot be truly known except by those who have gone through them. The heights one may know, may be realized only by one who has experienced the resurrection that comes afterward. During this time Carla had a 'death mask' that comes at a certain stage. The workings of the kundalini during this stage is as the destroyer. It destroys the ego nature, and to the degree we identify with the body and its relationship to the world, we feel we are being destroyed as well; this is the pain that will end all pains. With the crushing of the 'old cup' of consciousness comes the promise of a new cup, or as Jesus said it, "a new wineskin." But during this experience the new cup cannot be known; so only child-like trust can take one forward at this time.

A NEW CUP

What wondrous power awakens
Deep within my being
A power to change
A power to transform.

O mystic power of Kundalini,
So much promise lies in your awakening
So little does the pilgrim know
What torturous paths lead to that promise.

For your power is destruction and creation
And first you must destroy
To rid the consciousness of error and ego
To empty the cup of old wine.

That emptying means the crushing
Of the cup, and of all that remains of the past,
Becoming rid of all we cling to
As a dying person clings to every breath.

The crushing grinds to white all the stain
Of error-ridden past,
And breaks our grip
Of cherished notions of old.

So thoroughly do you destroy
That I have nothing to claim as my own
And if 'I and mine' raise objection
Your heavy grinding stone works it to dust.

On goes your work
Heedless of puny human groans,
For your work is Divine
And so your needs transcend the little 'I.'

But, your work is not merciless
And if in pain I cry out
You give comfort, strength and aid
To continue such a mighty work.

O Divine Kundalini
You are not the goal, but the answer to it,
But what a fantastic journey you embark us on
To attain our goal Divine.

What will be the end?
One cannot tell
But in faith and child trust
I follow where you lead.

In gratitude I bow to you
The worker of change and transformation,
In your work lies the pain to end all pain
In your work lies ultimate freedom.

So continue on in your work
Till all is ground to finest dust
To make a new cup of purest gold
To be filled with holy wine of Spirit alone.

India's Gift

This book of writings
Is dedicated
To the journey, nay a pilgrimage
Embarked on to holy India.

For India is the source of inspiration
Of these writings
Holy India, the ageless spirit of her soul
The vigor of her past, present and future.

India, with her saints of timeless past
Has bequeathed to us her wisdom
And selfless spirit
And her realized Masters that shed their Light.

It is through the gift
Of her peerless masters
Both ancient and new
That I have imbibed spirit's nectar.

And this nectar has flowed
Into picture-words
Of inspiration and upliftment
That sets my soul glowing.

These words have not come from me
But through me
They flow through me
As water flows in the river channel.

I know not their worth
Other than these words flow
From silent communion with the Infinite
And resonate with my deepest sentiments.

I pray that in reading these words
They bring you into communion

With that indescribable Presence
That is the source from which they came.

I pray the blessings of that Infinite source
Be received by you
And you may be a perfect reflection
Of its beauty, power and grace.

Lofty Peaks

Lodged at Ma's Dhaulchina (Cheena) ashram, atop a peak at seven thousand plus feet, we were told there were snowy Himalayan peaks just beyond the mist. Each day would play a game of hide and seek, as we would get glimpses of craggy peaks here and there. Finally, the morning after the most intense thunder and lightning storm I have ever witnessed we could see the entire expanse of mountains including the lofty Nandi Devi Peak. Then mists gathered and continued its game. Of course, we were mindful all the time that we were there to realize the unifying Consciousness beyond Its expression as those magnificent mountains. But the game of hide and seek seemed the perfect metaphor for seeing the Divine behind the misty veil of delusion. The delightful surprise to me was the refrain for the "Mother to teach us to love the game," to see the higher purpose in life at all times. As I witnessed these words coming through me I experienced the thrill of the game, the never-ending Joy the Infinite has in expressing itself as creation. To see the truth is real Bliss. May all come to realize that truth.

Peaks

You dance
Your dance
Of a thousand veils
Your game of hide and seek.

Daily, you dance your dance
Revealing and hiding

Showing and then not showing
Distant peaks of power and majesty.

O Divine Himalayas
O Mother of the Universe
How you love to play with your children
To tease, then to display in proud profusion.

You tantalize with a peak
Through a misty veil
Then remove another layer
And lo more depth and height is revealed.

Then dark clouds ramble in
And obscure vision of all but light
Through darkened veil come lightning flash
And reverberating thunder rolls.

Then morning breaks
And all veils are removed
Making measureless peaks
Radiate their purity of white.

Again misty veils obscure,
What was minutes ago
So bright and clear
And then a peak is seen to gleam.

O Divine Himalayas
O Divine Mother
How you love your game
How you love to play with your children.

Teach us to enjoy your game
Even as you enjoy it,
Teach us not to be attached
To our preconceived notions.

Let us play together
To wait in perfect anticipation
Then to explode in wondrous joy!
At your revelation of beauteous peaks.

You, who have waited eons
For thy children to awaken
Whose heart has broken
At their thoughtless cruel acts.

You, who have waited eons
For your children to play with you
In joy of original purity and love
And return your love glances.

Teach us O Mother
To love your play
And to see you behind every veil
And every change of scene.

Teach us O Mother
To love you, the creator
Above and beyond your creation
To join you in blissful love alone.

Teach us O Mother
To know you beyond all creation
And to love your play of shadow and Light,
Teach us O Mother.

May we always be in love with you,
May we never forget you,
May we love your play, without expectation
May we live evermore in your love and joy.

Uplifting Himalayas

Steep winding roads to Himalayan villages and places of pilgrimages inspired this writing. Dwarahat, Almora and Dhaulchina are just some of the names that bring to mind roads and paths contoured to the land. The treks up some dusty, stony paths challenged some in the party to their utmost limit. A temple, ashram or cave awaited our ascent, gifting us with purified vibration for the effort. Superhuman effort followed by upliftment is the nature of the pilgrimage, such is the nature of the spiritual path.

It is difficult to describe the subtle, but powerful uplifting influence the Himalayas have. All nature, in its pure state, has that transforming effect. But the Himalayas have it more than any other that I have experienced. Here nature and saints have combined the power of prakriti, God as creation, with Purusha, God as pure Spirit. The sensitive heart is the recipient of that blessed union.

Himalayas

Twisting, winding paths
Creep up through misty clouds
Taking pilgrims towards their vision
Of mystic transformation of soul.

The road bumpy
Hills steeper still
Testing patience and perseverance
And resolve in purpose.

Glimpses come of distant shrines
Shining brilliant
Against deep blue backdrop sky
Tempting pilgrims to continue their course.

Fervent prayers are sent
To chosen gods
For strength and fortitude
To continue on the ultimate quest.

Suddenly, vision breaks through
To see the shining goal
Resplendent in glory
And its pure origin maintained.

Bathing the soul
In permeating grace
Of saint's and nature's bounty
Changing mortal into immortality.

O Himalayan peaks
Reveal your inner peace,
Kindle a fire of renunciation
From lowly mundane distractions.

O Himalayan peaks
Unfold your transforming power
Make Divine love my all in all
And lift me to your lofty vision.

India's Treasure

There is no leaving India
For once she enters your soul
She is ever with you
A part of your living being.

What is this strange attractor
That takes one to a distant place
With different languages
Philosophies and customs?

Why travel where travel can be difficult
Where physical poverty
And wounds on the body of the poor
Makes the heart sorrow in compassion?

I can only say
It is the call of the soul,
A seeking of life's deeper treasures
Lying hid behind a varied mask.

For India is above all else
A land of contrasts
The highest of the high
The lowest of the low.

Babaji once said,
"Be wise like the ant,
Pick out only the sugar
Mixed with the grains of sand."

Look for the good
And you will find it
Look for the highest of the high
It is there.

For India is a land of treasure,
Not the spices and jewels of old
But timeless spiritual treasure
Revealed in times both ancient and new.

Realized Beings grace her soil
And lift the veil of separation
So we might see the world anew
In its sacred pristine glory.

India is a land of treasure
For those who have eyes to see
With sacred temples, samadhis
And saints bringing purifying grace.

It is a Grace of spiritual uplift
And guidance to gaining a realized state

It is a grace freely given
To all willing to pay the price.

And what is that price?
To surrender self and all
And give oneself totally
To the ultimate search of Verity.

It is the ultimate price
But for those willing to give
It yields the greatest harvest
And makes one rich in spiritual wealth.

It is not India's Truth only
But universal to all mankind
Yet it finds its highest expression
In so many who have trod her soil.

Sacred places
And men and women of realization
Make for suitable pilgrimage
And expand the soul, when the Soul calls.

But listen to this O Sadhakas
India's treasure lies in your heart
No time or space separates you
From that true inner knowing.

India's treasure lies in your heart
And in the heart of all,
It is the heart of all great religions
And colorful myths of old.

Listen in the stillness
Feel for that mystic movement
And you will hear its calling
And see its truth unfold.

With your heart and soul
Is your treasure
Waiting for you to open wide
Your patient, persistent search.

And if wide you open
You will hear India's ancient call
That brings to your remembrance
All that you have ever known.

India's truth is universal Truth
And its call may be heard by all
India's truth resides in you
And will lead you home again.

In gratitude I bow to you
Holy India of saints and temples
For you have helped awaken in me
The timeless truth that is your treasure.

May I ever be a worthy son
May we ever be worthy children
Of noble realized Truth
That is India's greatest treasure.

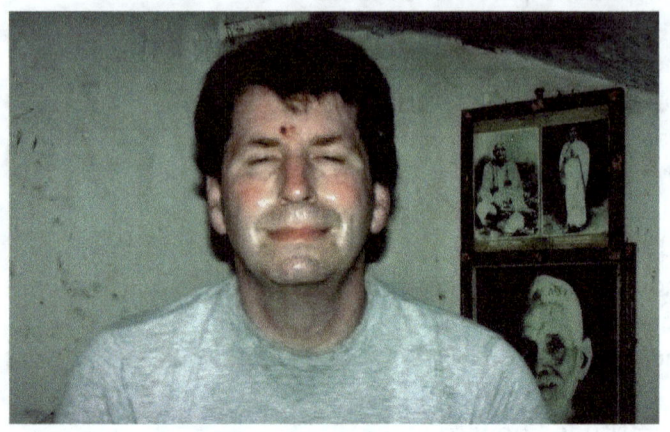

Yogacharya David, Ramanashram, S. India. 2005.

CHAPTER SEVEN: INDIA'S GIFTS

Ganges River at Dusk, Benares. India. 2005.

Yogacharya David and Carla, Camano Island, Washington, USA. 2015.

Chapter Eight
Mahasamadhi

Mahasamadhi is the dropping of the body or dying to this lifetime (in Vedic terms). David wrote of Mahasamadhi off and on during his long sadhana. Here, some early poems are interspaced with later ones. It does seem that David had some inner intimation of parting from this world and this dimension. In a poignant, soothing and uplifting poem found later in his journals, probably written in the mid-2000s, he says, "When I die do not mourn for this body . . . what I really am is not this jar of clay . . . I am the same life and intelligence that comes in the rising sun . . . so, hello my friend, a thousand million times hello, I am even now smiling in your heart."

In this section dedicated to Mahasamadhi, David's overall views of how life is Divine and separation is a delusion will be followed by specific homage to Swami Satchidananda. One year and seven days before Swami Satchidananda dropped his body, David wrote his *My Dear Ones* letter and what may have been his last poem, *Spirit Calls*. Did he feel that there was no point in "fighting the gravity that binds?" For David, that fateful day arrived August 12, 2019 when he dropped his body so he could better serve the Infinite One.

During his Memorial, David's beloved wife, Carla, read the eulogy that she has graciously given permission to share here. On David's first Mahasamadhi anniversary, Reverend Jill Hough and Reverend Peter Schultz offered the tribute included in this chapter.

We close with David's poem affirming how very thin the veils between realities are, once one is far enough up the mountain to ascertain with surety the real from illusion.

Enter In

To enter a family
Is to explore the Light and shadow
Of what it is to be human.

To enter the halls of Learning
Is to know the possibilities and Limits
Of the mind.

To enter marriage
Is to learn the meaning of commitment
And to become softer of heart.

To enter parenthood
Is to experience sacrifice
And Love unbounded.

To enter spiritual portages
Is to find who we truly are
And become one with the all embracing One.

To enter old age
Is to see clearly the cycles of Life
And learn the eternal youth of the heart.

To enter death
Is to leave this Little human cage
And face what we have created.

To enter into stillness
Is to become the great I AM of Spirit
And realize we have always been That.

Know Life and Death to be the Same

Know Life and death to be the same,
Living on earth is but a game.
Sorrow comes at separation
Know this to be delusion!

Look into your heart for your beloved,
And you will discover they are not really dead.
For there you find them living at peace,
For on life, they have a new lease.

Give up false ideas on how it is,
Know all life to be His.
Sometimes we fall asleep,
Wake up! And dive down deep.

When you have touched the heart of hearts,
You'll know no separation between parts.
Discover your true beatitude,
So much depends on your attitude.

A friend suffers because his sister died,
He thinks life is miserable and that it lied.
Know that she lives on even now,
She suffers no more under cancer's plough.

And if sorrow should creep into your heart,
Think her healthy, alive and tart,
For indeed she lives on today, encased no longer
In this mold of clay.

What is True Joy

What is the nature of true joy?
If all the nations call me blessed,
This is not everlasting joy.
But if all nations should revile me
And I stand unaffected,
One with God,
That, is true joy!

If friends and lovers
Should say sweet things,
Honor me with praise,
This is not enduring joy.
But if close intimates
Should betray me,
Seek to destroy me,
And I am forgiving in my heart
That, is true joy.

If I should have all wealth,
Success and fame comes my way,
Associates seek my favor and advice,
All the world, as it were,
Sits at my feet
That, is not unfading joy
But if fame and fortune desert me
And my love remains complete
That, is true joy!

If health and pleasure
Heaps their bounty upon me
And I say "life is good,"
This is not absolute joy.
But, if sickness visits me
Beauty fails me, old age overtakes me,
And residing in my Spirit I say, "life is good,"
That, is true joy.

If I were to lead a good life,
And at the end of my days
I enter the Heavenly Abode,
This is not supreme joy.
But if I were to live a life of slavery,
And at the end God should put me in hell,
And I saw some good I might do there,
And I felt gratitude to God for the opportunity
That, is true joy!

David wrote several poems in homage to Swami Satchidananda from Anandashram after Swamiji left his body. With the passing of Mother Hamilton, Swamiji became, as David says, his Second Mother. This beautiful enlightened and humble master nurtured the growing God-soul in David.

Goodbye My Dear

Goodbye my dear,
My beloved
Holder of my heart
Keeper of a sacred trust
Knower of deepest wisdom
God made manifest
Love personified
Fulfiller of my dreams
Guide to my fallen soul
Illuminator of my Soul
Goodbye my dear one,
My own.

Come

My dear Master
When you say with such love
I will come again, and yet again,
To save all souls from pain of separation
I hear a clarion call to all of us
"Come, come my brothers,
Come and bring your dear ones nigh."
One devotee takes the hand of the next,
That one stretches out and takes another
By their hand, and so on goes the chain.
It is a chain of humanity, a chain of love.
Come my brothers and sisters, come,
Come into the universal Kingdom of Soul
Where the Light illumines every mind
Where love is the only bond
Come to where wisdom sets the bearing
And service is the only activity.
Hear the Master's call dear ones
Hear his voice echoing through eternity
And come—come out of your darkness
Into the warm Light of Self-realization.

His Perennial Light

"The passing of a great One,
From his physical confines
Releases a spiritual Force
That blesses all the world."

The dearest of friends
No longer has a hand to hold
Nor eyes in which to gaze
No feet at which to prostrate.

I miss his presence already
Though I live at a great distance
The world itself misses him,
Knowingly or unknowingly.

An ache in my heart
Tells me something dear is gone,
A heaviness in being
Reveals an eclipse occurring.

Tears well up,
Goodbye my dear One
You have lit my Way
My deepest, deepest, deepest love to you.

Thus far
I have spoken of the lesser human
All of which is true
However, it is not all the Truth.

For there is another knowledge
Deeper—more profound,
Eternal
And all-pervasive.

With the death of a body
Comes a resurrection in Spirit
For those attuned to sacredness
With inner eyes to see and ears to hear.

The inner eye doth see
A shining and glorious Soul
Living free and joyous
All heart's desires fulfilled.

Spirit perceives Spirit,
Rising to love's greatest communion
No narrow limits remain
No sorrow can enter therein.

For joy follows upon joy
Blessed smiles radiate welcome
Personalities are transparent;
Doorways to omnipresent Bliss.

Life—life eternal
Obvious and without doubt
This truth reverberates forever more:
"Life is God and God is life."

Human and Divine
Are two perceptions under one Reality
Revealing a lesser and greater existence
An inner hand with an outer glove.

Human cannot stand alone
For separateness is suffering,
Suffering instigates desire for freedom
And freedom comes only from realizing God.

And this is what this great One taught,
This is what he lived,
This is what he aspired for all to know,
This is what made him great.

I bow at the feet of his wisdom
My heart blossoms in his love
I dive deep in his fathomless Soul
And I will forever soar high in his perennial Light.

A Fire Burns

A fire burns through the night
Searing the nerves
Purifying the dark waste.

Gathering other's karma
Taking it into the 3 bodies
Divine fiat alone declares this action.

The building darkness grows
Alleviating aspirants of their burden
Lightening their heavy loads.

O blessed night
Crucifies this physical form
A tapasya for others.

O heavenly Father
This is your compassion
Shown through this earthy shell.

You provide the means and the strength
As your servant shudders in the flame
You show your undying love through Your fire.

Over the years David reflected on his time here in this body and our time here on this planet. He wrote several poems reminding himself how we "come with nothing" and "leave with naught."

You Came with Nothing

You came with nothing
You leave with naught,
Possess you no things
Or have you forgot?

Clothes you have
And body too,
Things you save
But they have not you.

You are the center
And yours is the play,
All things come from within you
You have nothing to pay!

Poverty of Spirit
Poverty in flight,
A free bird has no nest
Not a place to light.

A heart unfettered
With the things of the world
Brings freedom to the Soul
So earns the greatest Pearl.

A Little Time on Earth

A little time I shall be on this earth,
A little time in eternity.
A little time of service to others,
A paragraph for infinity.

I follow Love's wisdom to the door,
I follow it to its end.
I follow Love's wisdom where e're it takes me,
I follow it around every bend.

Love blooms in springtime all 'round,
Love blooms in my heart of God's love.
Love blooms in the soul's garden year 'round,
Lightly it descends, softly as a dove.

Storms of desires gather their force,
Storms of desires send turbulent times.
Storms of desires shake the foundations,
Storms of desires run their course.

When God has finished His play,
When God has quit His fun,
Then God will call us back home,
And withdraw His Light 'n shade into One.

And then we will exist not as me and you,
And then we will not be apart.
But then we will know God as One,
And be even one with God, as we were from the start.

Death's Angel

Death's Angel often times comes unbidden
But, come he will.
At times he comes when old age
Signals, "It's time" like a
Clock chiming the midnight hour.
Other times he comes, it seems,
Too, too early, yet his timing,
Always impeccable.
Death's Angel is ultimately compassionate,
Though it may confound our logic.
And the release of a soul,
From this clay confinement
Is like the freedom of a newborn baby.

First Breath to Last

From first breath to last
This body lays claim to our attention
It is hungry—then full
Too cold—then hot
Happy to sad
Then happy once again.
It is a restless companion
Prone to activity and distractions
And yet—there is something more,
Like a secret it lures us past the obvious
It bids us to seek something,
The something is elusive
Yet feels intimately near.
Now we are warming to the solution
Quietly-quietly-quietly we go
Seekers are we
And the determined find
Those who give all

Receive all!
Quietly-quietly we go
The breath comes to rest
Truth reveals itself—once more.

On August 5, 2018 David wrote this letter to Kriyabans and it was published in *The Cross and Lotus Journal*:

> My Dear Ones
> There are times when I seem to be not quite of this world. In seeking to serve God and Gurus, I am finding They take me on diverse roads of Their own making. This poem below expresses some of what I experience, and what I most fervently want—that we all share in this heavenly kingdom that Mother, Master, Jesus, Babaji, and all great masters have come to inspire us to seek by sharing their Light with us. Even though I am not giving a talk this morning, know that I am with you in Spirit, and like the mariner in harbor who feels the power of the ebbing tide and first senses the wind that will fill his sails, so am I pulled out to the ocean of infinite bliss.

Spirit Calls

I soar upon wings of bliss;
Circumferenced never,
Open, clear, expansive, and joyful—
Oh what remarkable freedom is mine!

It is the bliss long-sought, a freedom hard-won.
How many years in the making?
How many tears shed in sorrow?
Only to discover the keys to freedom
Were in my hands all the time!

Now I soar and soar and soar,
Sometimes my feet touch the ground,
Other times I am borne in the air—
No tethers, no gravity, and no limits.

Whether of the earth or the air
I serve the Infinite One—
And with fire He scorches,
Removing ignorance from this world.

Dear ones, let us soar together;
Successfully fighting with worldly-gravity that binds,
And be as one with our infinite Beloved.
For even now, the Song of Spirit is calling to us all.

Truly as David shares, May the Song of Spirit call to us all. Om Tat Sat! The fateful day arrived and this Warrior of Light, Seeker of Truth did indeed loosen the tether, no gravity, no limits, David entered the world of the Infinite Beloved.

At David's memorial, Carla, David's wife and devotee, spoke these poignant words:

A Loving Tribute to Yogacharya David Hickenbottom
By Carla Hickenbottom

LOVE, that is what David was and is all about. When I first met him, I knew right away that there was something very special about him.

As my Guru, closest friend and husband, I have been privileged and blessed beyond any words that can describe to have been able to be with him for the last 25 years. He spent all the time we were together focused on bringing myself and all of you back to God, to knowing our Oneness with our Heavenly Father.

What was it like living with my Guru? I was asked that by Corliss at Anandashram and I answered, "Unfathomable." I knew that I was only experiencing a very small part of who David really is. He saved my life and all the years before meeting him was really preparation for my becoming his devotee but also his friend and life partner. All these years we were together and very rarely apart. Of course, different things came up but we really never argued, it was more about talking through what "worked and didn't work" in our relationship and sorting through the intricacies of living in the world. The only times he really got angry and let me know about it was when I wasn't doing my work, that I was afraid to talk to him out of fear or shame. He would say, I don't care how bad it is, as long as you talk to me about it, it will be okay. In the marriage vows, we really stressed to each other the importance of "forgiveness" and he taught me that time and time again through his example of loving kindness.

He used to say that the thing that made him the happiest was when the devotees did their own work.

He was fun, generous, kind, sweet, gentle, clear and had such a warm and engaging sense of humor. He would often say, "What's the fun!" He always loved how God presented new adventures for us and he would say that God would do that in the most "unexpected and delightful" ways.

While serving David in the body I was focused on his physical form and needs, and I knew and often experienced who he was in God. I now feel and experience the absolute true nature of all of his love, both human and divine.

I want to now tell you about what I witnessed and heard him say the last few days he was here. Up until the very end, he was still very present and when I would talk to him, especially the last few days, he didn't respond to me but then all of a sudden, I would say something and he would either whisper something or nod his head.

Seeing him lying there in the bed, I asked him, "What is the purpose of all this?" And he said, "To focus on God." He said: "God is beyond the light." "God touched me on the forehead." "JOY, JOY . . . why not?"

For about two days he had his eyes like Lahiri Mahasaya with the left eye half open and the right eye closed. He said he saw his circle of love expanding out from the room, the community, country and to all this world.

The day he left, God directed me to wash him in the holy Ganges water that had been brought previously by Jill. I took a white cotton washcloth and bathed him in this sacred water and chanted "God, Christ, Gurus" while doing so and the experience was so very blissful and extremely powerful.

On August 12, all afternoon and early evening, I felt that I couldn't stay in the room; it wasn't that I was being pushed out, or that he didn't want me there, it was more that it was just "too full" and Ruth helped me realize he was expanding more and more and into the Light of God.

I would like to end with what he had written to me for my birthday in 2014. Reverend Jill had made me a cardboard, fabric covered cake and on the large bottom layer, she had fellow devotees write short messages for my birthday which were so loving and thoughtful. On the top layer, in the smaller box were messages from David and I wanted to share these with all of you as I know that it is a gift for all of us:

> This world will always present us with reasons for feelings of loss, but the good news is there is a solution.
>
> When we surrender all to the Infinite Beloved, giving God our joys and sorrows, giving Him our all and laying it at His feet, and really letting it go, then He takes our burden and lifts it from us.
>
> When we empty ourselves of our sorrows, our loneliness, all that weighs us down, then He may fill that emptied cup with His bliss, peace and joy.
>
> Never forget, dear One, that you are made in His likeness and image. In your essence, you are a being of Light.
>
> When you look out through these two eyes and see only darkness, it is only a veil that has been drawn down around you. Look deeper, and you will see His Light shining in and around you.
>
> I have gone through darkness, through sorrow and feeling alone, I have felt the grief of the world, and I

know that God ever stands at the ready to lift us up, if we will let Him.

It is natural to feel such grief at times, but be sure not to nurture it, but give it to God. Do not be identified with it, but see it passing through you, breathing it through, letting it go. When you do this, it will pass, and God will come in and comfort you—this, I know.

Be at peace, dear One.
Surrender to God brings peace.
The surest sign of union with God is ever-new Joy.
Union with God is a deep connection with all humanity.
LOVE—is the one eternal constant.
Seva is love made visible.
God and Guru's blessings are ever with you,
In service—one to another—we are lifted higher and higher.

When David's first year Mahasamadhi arrived, sweet homage came forth as Reverend Jill Hough and Reverend Peter Schultz spoke at the memorial site.

Yogacharya Davidji's Mahasamadhi
(February 26, 1954–August 12, 2019)

Reverend Jill Hough spoke the following to attendees at Yogacharya David's first Remembrance Ceremony. She brilliantly selects a reading right from David as he honored the dropping of the body of a long-time devotee of Kriya Yoga, Christine. David initially, and now Jill, reminds us of how grand this multidimensional universe really is, and how little we know of the soul's journey. This is very poignant, as now David, too, is on his unique soul path traversing the worlds.

My Dearest Friends,
We gather today in gratitude and remembrance and to bear witness to our brother, friend, husband, teacher, guru and his dropping of the body through Mahasamadhi. I would like to read David's words on the marking of

the first anniversary of a beloved devotee's transition. It gives hope and direction for us all:

"Today marks the one-year anniversary when Christine left the body. What stands out clearly is that when a soul leaves this earthly existence, it leaves a void that cannot be filled by anything or anyone; life is simply not the same, nor will it ever be.

"As this realization deepens in me, it makes me more aware of how sacred life is; every life, everywhere. That search for the sacred, for divine healing was such a prominent feature in Christine, and what she inspired in many, many others.

"Last night we held a Service for Christine: reading from the Resurrection of Sri Yukteswar, I spoke, we then chanted and held silence. While in silence I beheld Christine in a striking inner vision: She was near a large waterfall, there were lush flowers and foliage all around, all was lit with a beautiful, spring-like sun and peace rang in the air.

"We communed in thought and in Spirit. My consciousness expanded like a geyser of radiance, transporting her into higher, more expanded awareness. As beautiful as the astral worlds are, they pale into insignificance in contrast to an experience in overarching Spirit.

"Then for some time we were again next to the waterfall. She exuded light and a brilliant smile. She indicated that she would wish me to pass on her love to all, and for no one to feel sorry for her, that she is happy and free of bodily pain and restrictions. The feeling of light and happiness comes easily and joyfully as I think of her now.

"There seems to be two realities, a physical one in which Christine has left a void of absence, and a spiritual reality in which she is ever-present and shining in a new world. Both are true, and while we deeply miss her, the greater reality is her eternal existence in

God. This is the key to all healing around the physical death of a loved one; while acknowledging the loss, we may also know the eternal existence of the Soul.

"What stands out to me in this moment is the tremendous feeling of love in my heart in thinking about Christine. And a feeling of fulfillment, that what she strove for in life—spiritual healing—has come to pass. Christine now has freedom from fear, and has found joy; freedom from aloneness and separation, and is joined into oneness in Spirit; freedom from disappointment, and is now content in Divine Love; she has a playground of all astral creation, that more easily accommodates her vast desire to create beauty!

"She earned all of these spiritual gifts by her relentless striving while here. Christine courageously faced her past demons, sometimes shaking and shuddering in the process, but never turning away from her path. And her expansive heart ever wanted to include everyone in the experience of growth; for she believed in, and eventually came to know, the real freedom and the lasting happiness that comes with bravely facing darkness in order to know the Light. This courage and tenacity for growth is what stands like a monument in Christine for all to emulate and follow."

Reverend Peter Schultz then read from David's writing:

My Dearest One,
When the world does not fulfill us, then we must turn our attention to God as our all and all. By staying focused on the world, we look to see how it falls short of our expectations and then we feel sad, lonely and betrayed. This is a burden and an expectation the world cannot fulfill.

So, put aside the things of this world—take your grief to God and surrender it at His feet.

Oh Lord, if You will not fill my heart by those around me, then fulfill me by pouring your Self directly into my heart and soul. Be the balm of Spirit that heals my lacerated Soul. Only You can make me feel whole. You have put me on this Spiritual Journey of oneness, and only You can make my happiness complete. I cancel my expectations for this world that I have carried for so long and I give myself to You, heart, mind and Soul. Spiritually free yourself from this burden. It is the material mind that thinks, "If I only had a different situation, then I would be happy." But is it so? God is with you in infinite Joy—why not find Him here and now?

With eternal love and blessings, David

At Yogacharya David's Mahasamadhi ceremony in 2019, Reverend Peter Schultz spoke of his own deep inner reflection.

The Courage of Acceptance

One of the great tenets of any spiritual path is acceptance of God's will. Some call it surrender, some call it bowing to your highest light, some call it listening to that still small voice within, and some call it acceptance. And it sounds great—right up until God hands you something you don't like, and don't want to go through. In the Christian scriptures the most dramatic example is Jesus in the Garden of Gethsemane when he implores God in Matthew 26:39: "O my Father, if it be possible, let this cup pass from me: nevertheless not as I will, but as thou wilt." Jesus knew full well what his enemies had in store for him—public humiliation, torture and death. And yet he said, not as I will, but as You will. That's acceptance. And it can be very, very difficult at times. But every spiritual master including our beloved Davidji tells us the same thing—it is an absolute necessity on our path to God.

None of us wanted to see David go now. At the time of his passing he was in his spiritual prime producing the most moving, most uplifting, most spiritually poignant messages of a long and beautiful dissemination of truth. He was our leader, our spiritual head, our counselor, our inspiration and our great example. How many things have you done where you thought—"Oh this would please David." We lived to make that man proud of us for one simple reason—he embodied goodness in our lives. And yet here we are without him. How does that make sense? The quickest reaction is anger. Why? Why did you take him, Lord? Why now? And then sadness, thinking of all the things we'll miss about him being right here with us. And in our anguish we strive to find solace in the only place we know—our inner sanctuary of God contact. And as we calm ourselves and gain that blessing, we feel peace. And though we may not know the exact reasons for our beloved Davidji's passing at this time, we know that it was perfectly orchestrated by the Master of All Things, for the greatest good of all. That's acceptance. Exactly what David wanted for us. And exactly what he demonstrated in the toughest situations—right unto the end.

We will close with a reflection from Yogacharya David for Mother's Mahasamadhi Day, Jan, 31, 2019.

> Just imagine in your own mind that you've come to the end of your life—everybody does—and it's actually a release, when the time is right . . . And you're ready to give up this body—it's served its purpose—and it doesn't make any difference what age you are . . . And just imagine—breathing out your last breath, and with it you expand out, without fear. You merge into the Light; you see that Light at the third eye point, and you rise up to the top of the head and you exit out of the body. And it's wonderful; it's freeing; it's expansive; it's peaceful; it's joyful; it's filled with Light—you're going

home. You're merging into your True Self. You don't have to split your attention between the material and the body, this world, and that Spirit that you have become one with. And so, you exit out of the body; you breathe your last; that tiny nerve in the center of the brain snaps; and you are released; you are freed.

When going through David's writings, journals and other materials after his Mahasamadhi, the following poem appeared—so potent—so absolutely profound and uplifting and wisdom-generating.

Smiling in your Heart (When I Die)

When I die, as all that is born must die,
Then do not mourn for this tomb of clay.
The body is but a small part of who I am,
And there is no sense in making it an idol.

When I die, there is a no more:
Ceaseless tides of breath,
Pounding of the heart,
And no more electrical circuits of brain and spine.

Know that Man is, I am, more than these body functions;
They are but extensions of life's creation,
But they are not life itself,
They are not the eternal Soul!

When I die, do not mourn for this body,
This "nest of troubles."
Who I am,
What I really am, is not this "jar" of clay.

I am the same life and intelligence
That comes in the rising sun.

I am not different than the spring breeze
Brushing against your cheek.

I have realized
The same life that expresses itself
Throughout creation,
Is also the life that is within me.

This I Am, may be for a time
A tiny bubble in the sea of creation,
And then that life-bubble bursts its bounds
And becomes one with the vast formless Sea.

It cannot be said the vast Sea is less than the bubble.
Yet, the bubble is now gone.
It has died.
And there is a definite change in that dissolution.

But that death is really just a beginning:
The beginning of a new stage;
A new life no longer encased in clay.
Learn to daily dissolve your tiny bubble,
And come, be with me in the cosmic Sea.
You may once again enter your little bubble of clay,
But never forget the fragrance of the infinite Sea!

For the same life that has inhabited this form,
Is now burning bright within you;
It is the same life that wafts to you in the flower's fragrance,
And the sun's reflected light in the morning dew.

Be at peace my dear one,
And feel me speaking even now in your heart.
Know that I am everywhere about you,
Loving you through all of life.

Life in this body is but a short span,
But the real Life is forever.

Join me each moment in that real Life,
And know your freedom, even as I do.

I would bid you goodbye;
But a farewell is only a tiny bit of the truth,
The tiniest part.
Yet, it must be said.

For I also say to you, "hello,"
In every breath you take,
In every delight you have in Spirit,
In the eternal life of our infinite Beloved.

You may say, "But you are gone!"
But this is just a game of a child.
In truth there is no coming nor going,
For Life cannot be created or destroyed.

So, hello my friend,
A thousand, million times hello!
I am, even now, smiling in your heart
And shining in lofty heavens!

Mount Temple, Alberta, Canada, by Dennis Brown (courtesy of the artist).

Yogacharya David, Utah Mountains, USA. 2018.

Chapter Nine
Aphorisms and Principles

David brings us affirmations, aphorisms and a set of principles for living. These succinct statements could be considered mantras and, as David says, can be utilized 'daily' and 'everyday.' If these precious words are taken as mantras, then the power they bring can become transformative. It appears that David used these phrases as a spiritual method, as a practice to support and sustain his climb. He uses well-known mantras in his prayers and poems such as OM and Om Sri Ram Jai Ram Jai Jai Ram, spiritually charged words chanted with sincere devotion silently or out loud in India for centuries.

The inner change comes from the information carried by the frequencies elicited from the words. These frequency waves can change consciousness and be used to harmonize disruptive states of being. In other words, we can use words in devotional chant form to decode old unhelpful perceptions or stuck lower-nature-mood states, and through our own initiative, rewire our perceptions and state of being to higher order perceptions and service, and to seek, as David says, unlimited Grace in God.

The realities crucial to the inner yogic path require adoration of the heart, clear discernment of the will, and understanding of the intelligence: all necessary if the sadhak is to attain the evolutionary self-seeing and soul state that transforms lower human emotions and motives to right relationship with the superconscious truth of Sprit. These sacred directives can support sadhaks to identify the personality built around a lower egoic desire-nature and its attributes, and initiate changes that create a healthy egoic state that willingly serves the higher vision for humanity and all sentient beings.

We start with daily affirmations.

Daily Affirmation

Every day I lovingly tend my field
I vigorously pull out weeds and tares
And throw them into the fire.
I tenderly sow only the highest quality seeds
And fertilize them with repeated effort.
I do this with a patience and persistence
That defies all logic.
And know that the results will come in their own time.
Every day I lovingly tend my field.

Every day

Every day I will work on perfecting myself in You.
Every day I will take steps rightly guided toward Your domain.
Every day I will surrender my efforts to Your Infinite Will.
Every day I am Your child, who knows I am loved and cared for.
Every day Your Light illumines me, and through me, the world is illumined.
Every day You live Your life through me.
And every day, You and I are One,
And blessedness reigns supreme.

Do All the Good You Can

Do all the good you can
By all the means you can
In all the ways you can
In all the places you can
To all the people you can
As long as you can.

You

O Lord, make my desire for You,
Greater than any other desire.
Make my love for You
Captivating and maddening.
And make my service to You
Perfect and pure in all I do.
Om Tat Sat

Remember

Let every lack prompt you to open wider the door to prosperity,
Let every darkness make your demand for Light grow in fervor,
Let fatigue remind you to open the floodgate of living Waters,
Let sorrow make you feel love enfolding and supporting you,
Let every ache and pain of the body make you see and feel healing forces
Washing away pain and discomfort,
Let every need make you know that God is calling on you to be a conduit for His unlimited Grace to flow through your prayer-demand.

Unlimited is God's Grace

Unlimited is God's Grace—it moves through you, out to manifest creation. You are His gateway—and you are the witness to His loving—joyful creative abundance demonstrated moment by moment, day by day!

Many have a love-hate relationship with money—others a desire-fear or other conflicting relationship with prosperity. You must heal your conflicting relationship before you can enjoy all that He is ready to give.

Make your first prayer-demand, "Oh Lord, open Your doorway of Grace to these places of conflict, making my hate, distrust, fear and anger disappear in Your Light of Understanding and Grace of Joy!"

It is not a matter of whether you have the funds for a particular desire or not—it is only important whether you feel it is for the highest good of all—in keeping with Divine Will. Once you establish your desire is for good, then place your prayer-demand to God—for He is waiting to give all His Good to you, now and always.

David asks us to remember. He tells us in his poems his prayer-demands and he shows us how faith is a sure guide. He pauses in his climb at times to fight inward battles—he brings out the spiritual warrior clearly commanding God to intervene to shelter him even as the demon grinds and tempts. David warns of how easy it is to slip down the slope, simple with desire-nature a sure ally—down is easy. Nevertheless, up is the Way, the Path to realization.

David's Param Guru, Yogananda (known as Master) in *God Talks with Arjuna: The Bhagavad Gita* speaks about the righteous battle, saying:

> Beholding the 'goddess of righteous duty' as she stands on the sacred altar of life, the spiritual warrior should not hesitate to accept his superior duty to rout out invaders of ignorance by fighting to acquire wisdom. Nor should a strong soldier, nurtured on the lap of his mother country ever waver in protecting her and safeguarding her worthy interest ideals.

Yogananda speaks of two kinds of noble warriors:
> The soldiers of the land who engage in a righteous war for the protection of their country, and the spiritual warrior who is ready to use self-control and undaunted endeavor to protect the inner kingdom of peace. No warriors of the Spirit should hesitate because of the delusive stratagem of the inner enemy.

He goes on to say:
> ... nor should a warrior avoid a righteous war against aggressors, protecting innocent, helpless people and preserving their noble ideals and freedom—is righteous duty.

Yogananda wisely continues:
> Good and evil are relative opposites in this world of duality. Good draws its power from the pure creative vibrations of Spirit; evil derives its force from delusion. The effect of delusion is to divide, agitate, and cause inharmony. Love is the attracting power of the Spirit that unites and harmonizes. When man (and woman) tunes in with God's love and consciously directs its vibratory force against evil, it neutralizes the power of evil and reinforces the vibration of good. Hate, vengeance, anger on the other hand, are of the same ilk as the evil being resisted, and so only inflame the evil vibration. Love smothers the fire by denying it fuel! God has shown me many times the power of His love in conquering evil ... Evil, by the judgement of cosmic law, writes its own death sentence ... the doctrine of nonviolence only works when the enemy's consciousness is capable of being touched. Though force in itself is an evil, when employed against a greater evil, the lesser of the two evils becomes in this world of relativity an act of righteousness. *(pg. 245–251)*

In this same text Yogananda cites Mahatma Gandhi's view that ahimsa (nonviolence) only works when the opponent's consciousness is high enough to understand the principle of nonviolence. If the opponent's conscious level is too low and intentions are evil, harmful, cruel, then running away or doing nothing is cowardice says Gandhi. Cowardice is the greater evil. The lesser evil is to take action to correct the ideal of right living.

David developed a series of aphorisms or statements of wisdom, brief phrases that he felt could provide guidance on the sacred path. His aphorisms are designed to keep the vibrational frequency high, enhancing internal harmony. Indeed, the aphorisms deny fuel to the negative while nurturing a sustained internal refinement of consciousness. This higher vibrational consciousness impacts external reality.

Aphorisms

Respect is the cornerstone of all relationships.

Over familiarity blinds one to the Divinity in another.

See the Light of God in all and appeal to that Light in all your interactions.

Attachment leads to anger, despondency, jealousy, fear and greed.

True love flows freely and demands nothing.

Love bleeds freely for another.

Real love can only stand on the rock of Truth.

One should live with eyes-wide-open intention.

Integrity results from clarity of seeing one's own self.

Fall once, get up once. Fall a thousand times, get up a thousand and one times.

Speak simply, plainly, truthfully.

Let also there be silence amongst you.

Be honest with others and be not deceived by others.

God alone is.

Think more, speak less.

Amongst activity, be inwardly still.

Follow your highest Light and trust in the Supreme Consciousness.

Forgiveness means to let go.

Lack of forgiveness ties you to the misdeed.

Discern what is true, but cast no stones.

Lack of dharma poisons the self and society.

The world requires every one of us to fulfill our destiny in order to be in balance.

The whole of humanity is made up of individuals; our destiny depends on every one of us, what we think, say and do.

Clear thinking requires a calm mind.

Peace comes from God.

Inner attunement brings life in abundance.

Desire nothing, all becomes available.

Constant remembrance of God purifies the mind.

Consciousness is a vast mansion with many rooms. Be not satisfied with a basement view!

Intuitive wisdom comes with an inwardly calm receptiveness.

God is the all-powerful, everywhere-present, ever-new

blissful Presence that equally resides in your heart and soul.

Be blissful!

Greed is a grasping closed fist. Be open and receptive like a flower in bloom.

Eat not to fullness. Make your stomach half full of food, a quarter full of liquid and a quarter air.

Let those things that grow in the earth be your food.

Life is the Light of man, and the focus absorbed in the Light brings life anew.

Each day is a new incarnation. Exclaim, today I create anew!

Become calm. Surrender to the moment.

Ask yourself, who is breathing, who has these thoughts. Go beneath the surface of things and discover the Self.

Become bold! Be your self.

No one can replace you. You are unique in God.

Do what you do as if you are the first and only one to have ever done it.

Give, as yonder cedar gives of its fragrance. Even in the splitting of its whole, so its sweet fragrance exudes more. Even as it burns! So does it breathe its last essence as a gift.

Do few things, but do them well.

Make your mark in silent craftsmanship.

Let your joy be in the doing, not in the results.

Act from your inmost Self, and let go of the rest.

Inwardly strive for perfection, knowing it is done by that which is already perfect within you.

You have courage enough!

Patiently Persistent, ever strive for the goal.

Right conduct today will ensure a better future.

Pay your debts with steady purpose.

Love leads you to your crucifixion and your resurrection.

Bear all difficulties with equanimity.

Life is meant to be lived in joy.

Fulfill your life's purpose each day, each moment.

Do not seek time to kill, but rather time to live.

God is nearer to you than your very breath.

Completeness comes from residing in your greater Self.

The affirmations and aphorisms are complemented by David's list of principles—each deserving of reflection and application.

Principles to Realizing God

To keep the focus of attention on God alone,

To love God with all the heart, mind, strength and soul,

To seek Truth without compromise,

To make every action a service to God,

To "be still, and know that I am God,"

In order to realize God we die to the ego to be born in the true Self.

Give of all that we are to be ever-filled.

Turn from the false in order to know the Light.

God is eternal existence, all-pervading Consciousness, ever-new Bliss
The Friend of friends
The nothingness of the uncreated
The most intimate of lovers
The impersonal witness
The power of all creation
The tenderness of the breeze on a flower-laden branch
The course of all intelligence and wisdom
The simpleness of a child

In short, God is the All in All
The Greatness of the great
The Purity of the pure
The all-consuming Beloved.

Standing at the Crossroad:
Questions to Ask at the New Year and Ongoing
(from January 1, 2014 Blog)

Review
What went right and why? Oftentimes we take for granted the things we have done well, as if there is nothing to learn from that experience. Take some time and review the things that have been positive in your year.

- What decisions did you make to create those positive outcomes?
- What can you do to build upon those positive decisions to create even better outcomes?
- Build a strong self-image according to those clear decisions and feel the strength it brings you.

What went wrong and why? Many times we fall into self-loathing, hide away from poor decisions or drown in self-pity. Instead take some time to view your decision-making from a learning perspective; wanting to understand why you made certain decisions.

- If possible, do what you can to make restitution or repair a bad decision.
- Trace the steps in making a poor decision, and find key moments of false logic or poor responses driven by emotion or desire nature.
- Recreate those key moments and see yourself making a wise decision, see it all the way through and experience how that feels. Then let that feeling reverberate all the way down to this moment as if that is exactly what you did. Let it change you to the molecular structure.
- Build a strong self-image for the present and the future based on making clear, wise and positive decisions. See your God-self fully manifest and guiding you, protecting you, and ever-present in your journey to Self-realization.

A New Year

A time for looking forward
A time for looking back,
A thoughtful time of assessment
A careful knowing of our track.

We celebrate the new year
We wave to the one that's old,
We make plans and resolutions
We close a chapter told.

What is this thing called Time?
But a progressive series of moments
That make up what we call 'our life'
We hope by end will bring fulfillment.

How quaint to chop and divide
How many moments we have,
How many months and days we share,
How we calculate eternity by multiple and then half.

Self is always eternal,
Self cannot be split,
Self is always present,
Self, ever-new, into clock and calendar
Alas, do not fit

David's affirmations, aphorisms and principles are each illumined through his poetic wisdom. Similarly, Yogananda in *God Talks to Arjuna*, offers guidance: "Though wisdom is superior to activity, still ultimate knowledge cannot be attained without activity. Social, moral, religious, and meditative action are all spiritual activities. They are different rungs on a ladder of salvation that every devotee must first climb in order to reach the illuminable sky of wisdom."

Each statement of David's warrants meditative reflection such that each becomes embedded into the deep psyche—each internalization will surely enable a successful climb up the sacred mountain.

Chapter Nine: Aphorisms and Principles

Arunachala Mountain, S. India, photo by Ruth Lamb, 2005.

Yogacharya David, 2011.

Chapter Ten
Closure

We have traversed almost forty-five years of the climb with David as he chose to share in poems, prayers and affirmations. Forty-five years of striving, of climbing, of dedicating his life to the Light, to the Divine ascent, the next evolutionary very-possible progression for human-kind. David represents one who is willing to make the climb and not stop even at the mountain top. He continues and he invites us to aspire and to climb.

To affirm the universal nature of this quest, here is a brief narrative outline as shared by Sri Aurobindo, in *The Life Divine,* describing the complexity and dynamic intricacy of such a climb, leading to the "fourth status of Life in its ascent to the Godhead."

> Humans, in proportion as they develop into a self-conscious and truly thinking being, becomes acutely aware of all this discord and disparateness in their parts and they seek to arrive at a harmony of a mind, life and body, a harmony of their knowledge and will and emotion, a harmony of all their members. Sometimes this desire stops short at the attainment of a workable compromise which will bring with it a relative peace; but compromise can only be a halt on the way, since the Deity within will not be satisfied eventually with less than a perfect harmony combining in itself the integral development of our many-sided potentialities. Less than this would be an evasion of the problem, not its solution, or else only a temporary solution provided as a resting-place for the soul in its continual self-enlargement and ascension. Such a perfect harmony would demand as essential terms a perfect mentality, a perfect play of vital force, a perfect physical existence. But where in the radically imperfect shall we find the principle and power of perfection?

Mind rooted in division and limitation cannot provide it to us nor can life and the body which are the energy and the frame of dividing and limiting mind. The principle and power of perfection are there in the subconscient but wrapped up in the tegument or veil of the power Maya, a mute premonition emerging as an unrealized ideal; in the superconscient they await open, eternally realized, but still separated from us by the veil of our self-ignorance. It is above, then, and not either in our present poise nor below it that we must seek for the reconciling power and knowledge.

Equally, humans, as they develop, become acutely aware of the discord and ignorance that governs their relations with the world, acutely intolerant of it, more and more set upon finding a principle of harmony, peace, joy and unity. This too can only come to them from above. For only by developing mind which shall have knowledge of the mind of others as of itself, free from our mutual ignorance and misunderstanding, a will that feels and makes itself one with the will of others, an emotional heart that contains the emotions of others as its own, a life-force that senses the energies of others and accepts them for its own and seeks to fulfil them as its own, and a body that is not a wall of imprisonment and defense against the world, but all this under the law of Light and Truth that shall transcend the aberrations and errors, the much sin and falsehood of our and others' mind, wills, emotions, and life-energies—only so can the life of humans spiritually and practically become one with that of their fellow-beings and the individual recover their own universal self. The subconscient has this life of the All and the superconscient has it, but under conditions which necessitate our motion upwards. For toward the Godhead seated in the sea of eternal light, in the highest ether of our being, is the original impetus which has carried upward the evolving soul to the type of our humanity.

> Unless therefore the race is to fall by the wayside and leave the victory to other and new creations of the eager travailing Mother, it must aspire to this ascent, conducted indeed through love, mental illumination and the vital urge to possession and self-giving, but leading beyond to the supramental unity which transcends and fulfils them; in the founding of human life upon the supramental realization of conscious unity with the One and with all in our being and in all its members humanity must seek its final good and salvation. And this is what we have described as the fourth status of Life in its ascent towards the Godhead ... where Consciousness and Force arrive at their own divine equation. *(pg. 230–231)*

In 2017 David wrote the following letter to sadhaks. It is personal and direct—it interweaves the human-to-divine trajectory. David could be sitting right beside us as he speaks. And he is saying in his own personal words in essence just what Sri Aurobindo is saying. They are both encouraging us to seek the greater path—the fourth status—and to welcome all that the journey requires to activate the Supraconscious Mind, an unbroken connection with the Divine.

> There are times in life when we question our purpose in living. Implicit in this search for meaning is the assumption that there is a purpose, even a very high one, in this rough and tumble existence here on earth. It has been the pursuit of many of a philosopher, and anyone who thinks on the deeper things of life, as to what might be the answer to this ageless inquiry. This question simmered in my own life from early on and became a burning need in my late teens. Back then I had no answers nor even many hints as where to look. So, I instinctively took the path of jnana-wisdom and eliminated what it was not.
>
> When I was a dozen years in age, I rejected the religion I was born into, acknowledging the greatness of Jesus the man, but unaccepting of Christianity

being the one and only way, and that all others were sentenced to eternal hell, damnation and suffering; this I could not accept as just or compassionate of any god or God. I considered the way of science for some time, and while I continued to hold it in high esteem, it quickly became apparent that it held the answers to many questions, but in the essentials to my quest, it admitted its inadequacy and sent me to the philosophy department. As I looked around at the people I knew—many fine individuals with good minds and leading virtuous lives, but I found no inspiration for what I could hang my hat on. And the thing is, this was not a casual inquiry done from the comfort of my armchair (which I did not have at the time.) In high school I paced like a caged animal; I was restless for who knows what—a something—something greater than what I had, what I knew, and what I saw.

It was only when I started reading about Eastern spiritual masters and Native American teachings that I felt a spark, a consuming interest that led me into new understandings. When I first read about reincarnation, I somehow knew that this was the truth, even though I did not have any direct memories of it. The evidence I had was my own inner knowing, and although not scientific, it was valid to me.

This intuitive knowing was to become my guide in so many of the adventures that lay ahead. Part of what intuition told me was that I was on the right track, but I was missing the essential part; reading books was not getting me to where I needed to be. That is when I read about a man meeting a guru. He described having tears, being bewildered, but knowing this was exactly right for him. I thought, "That is what I need, to meet someone who knows about what I am going through, who can help guide me in the proper direction, because right now I know something is missing, but I have no idea what!"

Following intuition brought me to my Guru, in a totally unexpected form as a Western woman. But that is the thing about intuition, it is a completely different means for knowing than the reasoning mind. Through her teachings my life was being purified and my intuitive faculties awakened even more. I was taken on journeys wholly new to me, directions I would have never gone simply following my reasoning mind.

I thank God and Guru every day for having and developing this faculty. There are those who completely discount intuition, but I do not think they have really given it a fair evaluation. There is plenty of reason to be careful using intuition, to discern what is true inner direction from "false prophets." Those "false prophets" of thoughts and feelings can come from many directions: our own prejudices, fears, desires, other people's influences, or deep subconscious impulses. To separate the wheat from the chaff requires we be completely sincere. Any hint of fear, greed or anger will taint intuition or completely supplant it with our own agenda. There are certainly times in life when a sudden insight hits us like a bolt of lightning without our cultivating intuition one little bit, however to make this inner knowing a reliable guide means we have to work at clearing our minds of those lower emotional impulses and preoccupations of the mind.

Given the difficulties encountered, one may dismiss the whole subject. However, the benefits of a developed intuition are too great to ignore. The subject of intuition can be limited to a psychic connection to another, sensing a coming event or seeing and hearing astral phenomena.

However, the highest and best use of intuition is to gain access to the Superconscious Mind, that faculty of intelligence that supersedes ordinary thought and reason or psychic perception and raises the level of consciousness to the realization of the universal nature of God.

The Psalmist said, "Be still, and know that I am God." Meditation makes the mind quiet, allowing us to hear the "still, small voice." It is only called "small" because it often comes in a very quiet way. Too much noise of the ordinary mind renders it unheard. That is why emotions and thoughts need to be suspended; only then are we still enough to hear and to know God.

It may sound audacious to some to say we can know God, but that is exactly what the world's greatest teachings proclaim. Jesus said all that he did, we may do as well, and even greater things. And, the Vedas say, "Arise, Awake!" It is time; a new, greater realm of existence awaits us to explore its many wonders and beauties through soul awakening intuition that will guide us to our true purpose.

David has shared with us in beautiful poetry how he responded to the call. He has shared the fierce purification process as he fought for the Truth, as he literally tackled his lower consciousness and forced it to surrender to a higher light within his being. He brought forth the true submerged and the true heightened consciousness. He refused its concealment in false ego and lower desire nature, habit and old programs. He clearly examined his desire nature, his vital cravings, his satisfactions and his repulsions. He witnessed his thoughts, his mental play, his perceptions and deceptions, and his rationalizations. David worked with amazing sincerity to remove veils of ignorance and falsehood. He fought for views of his universal force and of his divine nature. As his knowledge grew, his self-mastery while slipping down the mountain on numerous occasions, as he shared, eventually triumphed more and more. He was compelled to discover the deity inside, seated within him. In his Homecoming, he sought his greater being.

David refused to stop. Remember, his was a forty-five year journey: living in a positivistic, materialistic, commodity-driven five-sense, external-oriented world, explicitly designed to keep the human spirit in slavery to senses and the external. David removed falsehood after falsehood, wrapping after wrapping, joyously sometimes and in pain other times, but ceaseless the climb! He learned that " . . . as the Consciousness is, so will the Force be."

David gave us the tools, and revered masters throughout time have affirmed practices: we have enough gear! We can climb! David remains ever with us in joy exclaiming:
"Look Upon the Mountain High!"

Look upon the Mountain High

Look upon the mountain high,
Climb straight up, don't be shy.
Feel the earth on your bare feet,
Keep on going, never know defeat.

Nightly streams of water running,
Recognition of its conscious murmuring.
Move on up the mountain high,
Don't stop, don't die.

Burning sun running through your veins,
Fire purifies and causes pains.
Keep on climbing, its vital now,
Pain and anguish are part of the Tao.

Freedom now in the sky,
Watch out! That's just a lie.
Wake up, don't be carried away,
This is not where you're supposed to stay.

Keep on climbing though it's steep,
You're almost to the peak.
The Perfect Master is now in view,
Look upon him, you know what to do.

The all-pervading sound is now a roar,
Relax, this Word is the door.
Colors abound and turn into one,
Blue is all around,
Now look to the Sun.

Here it comes in bright streaks,
Like a sun coming over a peak.
Then it bursts upon you as the one,
The trip is over, you are done.

Becoming one with the Light,
You end your intense plight.
Now if it is to be, you come back to Earth,
Be careful don't lose your mirth.

Loneliness descends as you come down,
Joy will return, you need not frown.
Spread the message far and wide,
You have seen God's side!

The Expanding Path, photo by Michael Victory, 2009.

Yogacharya David, 2011.

"When there is a dedicated core number of souls in this world emulating universal love and service, by even a fraction of what is done by the Masters, then this world will be changed in radical and beautiful ways ... The main thing is to keep one's mind upon the Divine. Through constant God-remembrance the mind is purified and is lifted into the divine realms."

—YOGACHARYA DAVID

Acknowledgments

Yogacharya David made this book possible. He gifts us as he shares experiences in poetic form—experiences that traverse a forty-five-year sadhana journey of spiritual progress.

A very special thanks to Carla, David's life partner and devotee, for trusting me to compile her beloved husband and Guru's life work, and for sharing David's photos so generously. She also has agreed to the sharing of her memorial tribute to David and personal experiences as David outlines in the book.

Thank you to Reverend Larry Koler and his wife Cate Koler for their long-term ever-present commitment to sharing Yogacharya Mother Hamilton and Yogacharya David's teachings. And on that note, a beautiful thank you to Reverend Jill Hough and Reverend Peter Schultz for standing strong sharing the Kriya Yoga teachings.

Artist Dennis Brown gifted us with an image of his *Temple Mount* painting, and photographer Michael Victory used his photographic skills to refine some of the images and he provided us with a beautiful mountain photo—thank you both.

Thank you to Carol Sill, my editor and book designer for the first edition, for her patience, inspiration and understanding as we worked together deciding how best to feature David's precious poems. Jan Westendorp of Kato Design and Photo brought her artistic and book design expertise forward to assist in the development of this reprint.

Index of Poems

All poems are ordered by chapter and include the date written if available.

Introduction
I Am (September, 2002)

Chapter One
The Call and The Response
Arise, Awake (September 27, 2000)
Awaken Me O Divine Mother (September 18, 2000)
Black Clouds of My Divine Mother (undated)
Blessed Lord (undated)
Blessed Lord Let Me Be Thy Instrument (Undated)
Devotees Test: There is a Mountain to Climb (January-February, 1997)
Divine Search for God (August 23, 1995)
Feel God's Presence in Every Cell (August 30, 1996)
Hear the Savior's Call (April 13, 1997)
Hide and Seek: Be Gracious Now (undated early)
I Am Your Instrument (May 18, 2013)
I Walk Alone, I Walk and Walk (1978)
Inner Pain Was My Master (August 30, 1996)
It is You Lord (January 19, 1997)
Just for Today (September 12, 2000)
Lonely Feelings in My Heart (1978)
Morning Jewel (January, 1997)
My Hari is Near (December 16, 1977)
O Beautiful One in my Heart (1978)
O Great Spirit of All (1978)
O Lord My Comfort Come to Me (February 2, 1997)
O Lord my Love for You is Incomplete (February 18, 1997)
O Master Engraver, Lift Me Up the Mountain (1978)
O Sadhakas (undated)
Power Surges (2002)
Spiritual Sleep (1978)
Sweet Misery You Are My Friend (undated)
Tell Me My Lads (1997)
Through Trials I Grow (1978)
You Have Asked Me to Teach (January 17, 2005)
Your Will (September 28, 2000)

Chapter Two
The Path of Purification

Anger's Quest (2006)
Assailed by Delusion's Plight (1978)
Be a Slave of the Senses No Longer (1978)
Blessed Lord I Feel Your Presence (1978)
Body Perfections (2006)
Cast Off Your Mask of Duality (1978)
Dark Ghosts Become Angels of Light (2006)
Darkness (April-June, 1999)
Destructions End (undated)
Don't Let My Mind Go Astray (1978)
Faith Out of Sight (1978)
From Sense Drunk Life, Back to the Sea (June 16, 1996)
God Suffers (undated)
I Did You a Wrong, I Know that Now (1978)
It Is You Alone (est. 2006)
Look Upon the Mountain High (1978)
Make Me Yearn for You (June 6, 2008)
Misery—Get Behind Me You Have No Power (est. 2006)
My Sovereign Lord (July 28, 2014)
O Humility (1978)
O Lord How Long Will I Stray? (June 26, 1996)
Purification (March 3, 2002)
Regret Remorse Forlorn (undated)
Sadhana (undated)
Sorrow's Centre (undated)
Stand Valiant (1978)
Surrender to Grace (March 25, 2002)
Tears (1990)
Tears are Running Down my Cheek (1978)
The Seed that Yields Fruits (September 28, 2000)
There Is No Profit in Being Sad (1978)
To Now (est. 1978)
Transform your Urges, Don't Fall (1978)
Until (October 28, 2011)
Walking the Razor's Edge (est. 2000)

Chapter Three
The Path of the Witness

A Golden Alchemy (December 28, 2004)
A New Day (July 8, 2002)
Angels Sing (2000)
Breezes Blow (September 8, 2000)
Dance Divine (1978)
Devotees Come (May 29, 2008)
Fear to Peace (May 24, 1997)
Four Lions and The Diamond Light (est. 2000)
Good Morning (undated)
Great Builder of Images in the Mind (1978)
Hear My Prayer (undated)
I Am the Witness (January 12, 2003)
In the Beginning (2006)

Infinite Is Infinite (October 13, 2000)
Let Go, Let It Be (August 19, 1996)
Look for the Light (1978)
Lost at Night (2006)
Love Flows all Through and Through (1978)
O Friend of Friends (November 5, 2000)
O God of My Heart (1978)
O Infinite Compassion (January 15, 2005)
O Infinite Joy (March 25, 2002)
O Infinite Presence (December 29, 2006)
O Infinite Self (January 9, 2005)
Sacred Language of the Gods (January 9, 2005)
Seducer of Souls (April, 2003)
Silence is Golden (October, 1999)
Smile that Everlasting Smile (1978)
The Flower Glories in the Sun (1978)
The Light Bearer (November, 2008)
The Shepherds' Watch (2011)
The World Stood on Its Head (undated)
Truth Comes in Hidden Ways (July 7, 2000)
Two Paths in the Wilderness (2011)
We the Children of the Infinite (November 5, 2000)

Chapter Four
Homecoming

A Mystic Embrace (December 27, 2004)
A Voice Rang Out (undated)
All Glories be to You My Lord (1978)
All in One (July, 2000)
At Every Turn—Beauty (October 26, 2004)
Awakening (November 15, 1997)
Crystal Devotion (1978)
Flowers of My Dreams (September 25, 2000)
God is the Beautiful (September 12, 2006)
Hail to the Infinite (October 7, 2004)
Hail to Thee (January 15, 2012)
I Saw an Angel Today (1990)
I Stood Upon a Rock (undated)
In God Is My Abundance (undated)
Let Your Will Reign Supreme (October 22, 2000)
Light of the World (1998)
Lord Reveal Thyself (undated)
Miracles and Mariners (September 4, 1996)
My Purnima Moon (2011)
No Bubble Only Sea (August 10, 1996)
O Divine Mother Your Spirit is Universal ((December 6, 1998)
O Unfathomable Lord (January 24, 2005)

Sadhakas' Home Coming (undated)
Shining Grace (1998)
Shining Like a Tiny Sun (undated)
Song Eternal (January 29, 2002)
The Lord's Day (undated)
The Lover (2011)
The Vibrant Name (undated)
Thou Art Ever With Me (undated)
Universal Vision (April, 2003)
Upon a Golden Sea of Silence (November 23, 2002)
Upward Beauty (July 2, 1990)
What Presence Moves Within (July 8, 2000)
Yearning (2000)
You are Purna (January 24, 2005)
Your Light Illumines (2005)

CHAPTER FIVE
PRAYERS

Absorbed (September 21, 1999)
Be My Guide (May, 1998)
Coming Through the Darkness (1998)
Cure Me of Ego (1998)
Four-Fold Blessing (May 1, 1990)
I Know We Are One (September 19, 1999)
Make Me Free in Thee (September 16, 1999)
Make Me Know Thee (undated)
Make Me One with Thee (March 10, 1996)
O Creator of My Heart's Desire (July 8, 1998)
O Infinite Light (January 24, 2005)
O Joy Inexpressible (February 22, 2005)
O Lord (July 8, 2000)
O Lord Make Yourself Known (undated)
O Lord Protect Me (December 5, 1998)
O Mighty Supreme Spirit (October 26, 2000)
Prayer (September 9, 2000)
Prayer for Light (undated)
Prayer for World Enlightenment (undated)
Prayer to Divine Mother (1997)
Teach Me to See That It Is You (1998)
The Shining Sword Revealed (1998)
Thou and I (October 11, 1997)
Your Child (undated)
Your Child Nityananda (January 19, 2005)

CHAPTER SIX
GURU TRIBUTES

Awake My Infinite Children (March, 1996)
Baba (March 28, 2002)
Behold Divine Mother (1978)
Beloved Baba (September 21, 1999)
Bless Mother Tonight (1990–2)
God and Gurus (1998)
Guru is Your Heart (October 24, 2001)
Love's Ways are Strange (undated)
Maha (undated)

Mother is My Master (1978)
Mother, Master, Saints and Sages All (1998)
Mother's Cross (February 19, 1999)
Mother's Day (1978)
O Infinite Babaji (September 26, 2000)
O Infinite Papa (1998)
O Krishna (October 22, 1999)
O Krishna in My Heart (1978)
O Krishna the One and the Many (1998)
O Ma (March 29, 2002)
O Mataji (1998)
OM Mother (undated)
Our Beautiful Master (March 7, 2012)
Papa All-Pervading Presence (January 23, 2005)
Papa's Presence (1998)
Swamiji (1998)
Swamiji's Grace (March 12, 2002)
Through the Master (1988)
Thank You Babaji (February 21, 2005)

Chapter Seven
India's Gifts

A New Cup (March 23, 2002)
Anandashram Flower Ceremony (February 3, 2005)
Grant my One Request (1998)
Himalayas (March 19, 2002)
India's Gift (March 23, 2002)
India's Treasure (April 1, 2005)
Mandir's Freedom (February 2, 2002)

O Swamiji (February 2, 2005)
Peaks (March 23, 2002)
Silence (undated)
Song Eternal (January 29, 2002)

Chapter Eight
Mahasamadhi

A Fire Burns (October, 2008)
A Little Time on Earth (March 22, 1990)
Come (August, 2008)
Death's Angel (undated)
Enter In (September 9, 2000)
First Breath to Last (undated)
Goodbye My Dear (February 26, 2007)
His Perennial Light (October 15, 2008)
Know Life and Death to be the Same (1978)
Smiling in your Heart (When I Die) (undated)
Spirit Calls (August 5, 2018)
What is True Joy (October 2, 1999)
You Came with Nothing (1978)

Chapter Nine
Aphorisms and Principles

Aphorisms (est. 1999–2000)
A New Year (December 31, 1997)
Standing at the Crossroads (undated)
Daily Affirmation (April, 1997)
Do All the Good You Can (est. 1990)
Everyday (October 18, 2000)

*Principles to Realizing God
(1999–2000)
Remember (2005)
Unlimited is God's Grace
(undated)
You (1998)*

CHAPTER TEN
CLOSURE
*Look upon the Mountain High
(1978)*

Bibliography

Paramhansa Yogananda. (1946). *Autobiography of a Yogi*. New York. The Philosophical Library.

Paramhansa Yogananda. (1995). *God talks to Arjuna: Bhagavad Gita*. Los Angeles, California. Self-Realization Fellowship.

Sri Aurobindo. (1995). *Essays on the Gita*. Twin Lakes, WI. Lotus Press.

Sri Aurobindo. (1990). *The Life Divine*. Twin Lakes, WI. Lotus Press.

Swami Sri Yukteswar. (1949/1963/1990). *The Holy Science*. Los Angeles California. Self-Realization Fellowship.

Yogacharya David Hickenbottom. (2007). *Lahiri Mahasaya: Father of Kriya Yoga*. September Retreat Loon Lake. Canada.

Yogacharya David Hickenbottom. (2017). *Dear Friends*. The Cross and The Lotus Journal. March. Vol 18, #1.

Yogacharya David Hickenbottom. (2018). *Swami (Papa) Ramdas*. September Retreat. Loon Lake. Canada.

Yogacharya David Hickenbottom, D. R. (2019). *My Spiritual India*. Seattle, Washington, USA. The Cross and The Lotus Publishing.

www.crossandlotus.com

www.anandasharm.org

www.anandamayima.org

More information on
The Cross and The Lotus can be found at
www.crossandlotus.com

www.ingramcontent.com/pod-product-compliance
Lightning Source LLC
Chambersburg PA
CBHW052131070526
44585CB00017B/1784